The Developing Child in the 21st Century

The Developing Child in the 21ˢᵗ Century is a fascinating exploration of how ideas about childhood have changed over time and place. By introducing the work of the best-known theorists of child development, the author critically discusses and evaluates new and relevant global debates in this constantly emerging field, including:

- the child as 'active constructor of meaning' – focusing on the pioneering work of Piaget and Vygotsky;
- how the child really learns about the social world through social interactions;
- the perceived importance of play in the developed world;
- the significance of culture, and how children learn how to play the different roles they need to perform throughout their lives;
- the current emphasis on the findings of neurological studies in relation to child development.

Adopting a framework which includes sociological, cultural, anthropological, political, economic and historical views, this indispensable text sets out to paint a more global picture of childhood, and accurately describes the kind of life that is experienced by children right now, not only in the developed world but in many different countries and cultures. Teachers, lecturers and students taking courses in early childhood, psychology or sociology will find this essential and highly accessible reading.

Sandra Smidt was Director of Undergraduate Programmes in the School of Education and Community Studies, University of East London. She is the author of *A Guide to Early Years Practice* and *Observing, Assessing and Planning for Children in the Early Years*, both published by Routledge.

D1350449

The Developing Child in the 21st Century

A global perspective on child development

Sandra Smidt

Routledge
Taylor & Francis Group

LONDON AND NEW YORK

First published 2006
by Routledge
2 Park Square, Milton Park, Abingdon, Oxon OX14 4RN

Simultaneously published in the USA and Canada
by Routledge
270 Madison Ave, New York, NY 10016

Routledge is an imprint of the Taylor & Francis Group, an informa business

© 2006 Sandra Smidt

Typeset in Garamond by
GreenGate Publishing Services, Tonbridge, Kent

British Library Cataloguing in Publication Data
A catalogue record for this book is available from the British Library

Library of Congress Cataloging in Publication Data
Smidt, Sandra, 1943-
The developing child in the 21st century, a global perspective on child
development / Sandra Smidt.
      p. cm.
    Includes bibliographical references and index.
      ISBN 0–415–38569–5 (hardback : alk. paper) — ISBN 0–415–38570–9
(pbk. : alk. paper) 1. Children. 2. Child development. I. Title.

HQ767.9.S625 2006
305.231—dc22
                                                            2006002924

ISBN10: 0-415-38569-5 (hbk)
ISBN10: 0-415-38570-9 (pbk)
ISBN10: 0-203-96888-3 (ebk)
ISBN13: 978-0-415-38569-5 (hbk)
ISBN13: 978-0-415-38570-1 (pbk)
ISBN13: 978-0-203-96888-8 (ebk)

My father, Harry, my friend, Hilda, and my aunt, Gessy, all dreamed of a more just world. This book is in their memory.

Contents

Preface

In 1996 I was in South Africa and became involved in working for a project on early childhood education. This was in the early days of the post-apartheid government and the project was aimed at defining the minimum norms and standards that could be required of those working with children of pre-school age. I was delighted to be involved in this project and came to it full of the confidence I had gained in the UK as an early childhood 'expert'. I had worked as a teacher and a headteacher, as a local authority inspector and as a lecturer in education at more than one university. Early in the project I was asked to work with a South African colleague looking particularly at what we would include in our programme about children's learning and development. For me this was clear. We would need them to think about the work of the great theorists – people like Piaget, Bruner, Vygotsky and others. For my colleague, Ann Short, we would need to take account of factors I had not before considered – things like nutrition, health and poverty. Although I was, of course, aware of the impact of these on children's development I was firmly rooted in a Western psychological tradition and it took three days of constant, intense and furious discussion for us to agree to pool our expertise, our experience and our philosophies to come up with a less narrow view. It was from this life-changing experience that the idea of this book arose. So the book is an attempt to re-examine what we now know about how children develop and learn, taking account of a range of perspectives and ideologies.

In writing the book it was difficult to find a term to define what constitutes countries like England or France or the US as opposed to countries like South Africa or China or Peru. In the literature some authors refer to North and South, with the North referring to Europe and North America, for example, and the South to countries like South Africa and so on. Other writers prefer to talk of the majority and the minority worlds, with the majority world applying to the poorer countries and the minority to the more wealthy. I have chosen to refer to the developed world and the developing world, although these are not strictly accurate terms. It is clear that if one includes countries like China or Nigeria or Mexico, for example, in the developing world one implies that these countries are not developed and that, of course, ignores centuries of development. I use these terms, really, to define the privileged and powerful blocks of Europe, North America and the United Kingdom as opposed to the often poor, often repressed and often ignored countries.

In writing the book I have sought to discuss concepts that are sometimes difficult to explain and understand, and to use as many examples as I can find to illustrate these concepts in order to make them more accessible to readers. There is always a tension between academic writing and accessible writing and like many authors I try to bridge this divide. As an educationalist I am also concerned to offer models of learning for those reading the book and have chosen to revisit themes throughout the book. So you will find reference to concepts like 'intersubjectivity', for example, in the least expected places. As you are reading you might feel irritated at finding something that feels familiar to you in a new context. I hope you will accept that this is a technique to try and make the links between ideas more transparent.

I have very much enjoyed writing this book because it gave me the opportunity to bring together some of the themes that have dominated my personal and my professional life: an abiding interest in children and childhoods; an extreme anger at injustice, oppression and poverty; and a passion for the work of writers, painters, theorists and others who have worked and continue to work to improve the world for those who will inherit it.

Sandra Smidt
November 2005

Chapter 1

Children and childhoods

In this opening chapter we examine what is meant by child development, which leads us to look at how important both history and culture are to any understanding of child development. We will start by looking at childhood as a concept, and examine its origins and the importance of thinking about childhood as a space or a phase separate from adulthood. As we do this we will also look at how concepts of 'the child' have developed and how they do not remain static over time or place. Closely allied with concepts of childhood per se are aspects of reality such as poverty and rights and we touch on these. We develop a workable image of the child of the twenty-first century and touch on the notion of 'good parenting'.

Child development: Which child? What development?

It is evening in the Zocalo in Oaxaca in Mexico. The street sellers and the shoe-shine boys and the mariachi are out in the streets. Three-year-old Cristina is there, too, as she is every day and every evening. Her mother has a stall which sells plastic inflatable toys and giant balloons, which billow above the stalls in the breeze. Cristina is cruising the streets, as she does every evening. All the stall holders and the food sellers and the musicians know her: she is a member of the market community that inhabits the square. As she roams around munching on bits of food given to her, chatting to people, looking at the things on display she keeps her mother within view although she is perfectly safe. All the adults there treat her as though she were their child. This is her world. This is her childhood.

In Ho Chi Minh City, Hung is in the arrivals hall of the airport. He holds up a card on which his wares are displayed – books of postcards of Vietnamese scenes, bracelets made of strips of plastic, comic books. It is 2.30 in the afternoon and his school day has ended. He goes early in the morning and finishes in time to get in a whole afternoon's selling – and, more importantly, speaking English – at the airport and in the streets. He is seven years old and his English is fluid and fluent. He tells people he has learnt it from the tourists who arrive at and leave from the airport. He is known to the other sellers at the airport and to the taxi drivers and to the police who threaten to move him on, but his cheery smile seems to protect him from authority. He says he is saving up the money he earns (after he has given most of it to his mother) to buy a mobile phone. This is his world and his childhood.

Rian is two years old and lives with his mother, father and sister in a house in North London. He started going to a playgroup a few months ago and after a little trouble parting from his mother he soon settled down and loved the opportunity to play with other children; to sing songs and play musical instruments; to run around energetically in the outdoor space and to listen to stories and look at books. He loved the big toys outside and the sand and water and, especially, using paint and clay. His mother doesn't like him to get too messy at home. Last week his mother decided not to take him to the group any longer. She had read a report by Penelope Leach which said that the best childcare for children was with their mothers. So Rian now spends each day at home with his mother. This is his life and his childhood.

Lindelwa lives in KwaZulu Natal in South Africa. She is five years old. Her mother died of HIV/Aids last year and she hasn't seen her father for many years. He works far away. Her older brother Vusi is sick and so is her uncle. Three people in the house next door have died of Aids. Lindelwa lives with her grandmother and she goes to school whenever she can. It is a long walk to school but Lindelwa loves going to school and she wants to get an education so that when she grows up she can become a doctor and find a cure for the terrible illness which is devastating her community. Her grandmother thinks this is a wonderful plan and she has talked to the teachers at the school and they say they will help Lindelwa in every way they can. Hers is a difficult childhood and a difficult life.

Four different children: four different childhoods. This can be multiplied and multiplied and one would still not have any real sense of just how individual and different childhoods are. This is a book about child development. You may question why another book about child development is needed. After all there are dozens in existence, from the famous classical texts of researchers and theorists like Piaget and Vygotsky to simpler primers written for a range of audiences. This book aims to explore many of the ideas of the authors of some of those books and to consider how they contribute to our knowledge of children today, not only in the developed world but also more globally. This is a book which adopts a position that goes beyond the psychological and the individual and considers findings from other fields and domains which contribute to our understanding of how children progress in both the developed and the developing worlds. A consideration of child development at the start of the twenty-first century cannot afford to ignore the realities of life for the majority of the world's children. We start by considering what we mean by 'child development'.

Superficially, child development can be described as a discipline that looks at how children develop from birth (or even before that) to the end of childhood. The definition of when childhood ends, however, is not as simple as it might appear. In the Convention on the Rights of the Child childhood is deemed to end at the age of eighteen unless, under the law applicable to the child, majority is attained earlier. Child development is a discipline which aims to identify, to describe and to predict patterns in children's growth where growth includes intellectual (or cognitive), linguistic, physical, social, behavioural and emotional development. In other words, development is conceived of as holistic. Important themes emerge from this and embedded in these are a number of assumptions:

1   Since development is seen as *holistic,* all aspects of development are conceived of as being interrelated. The implication of this is that something that affects one aspect

of development may affect others. For example, children who fail to thrive physically are sometimes expected to fail in other areas. In some cases this is so but the question is whether this is a given.

2 Development is thought to be *continuous and cumulative* and the early years are almost always described as vital to later development. For example, children who have a difficult start in life are often expected to be less likely to succeed later in life. Again, there is evidence to suggest that this is often the case, but as the next point illustrates it is not always so.

3 Development is sometimes considered to have a certain *plasticity* which allows for children to adapt and adjust to adverse events and circumstances. Evidence suggests that some children who have a difficult start in life overcome enormous difficulties, and conversely children who have a privileged start to life sometimes struggle to adapt to later hardships.

Development, then, is a complex and dynamic construct and is sometimes described as though it exists outside of history and culture. The theme of this book is that development cannot be fully understood outside of a historical and cultural context. Criticisms are often made of the books written about child development on the basis that they adopt an almost totally Western view of children and of their development. When one considers that there are significantly more children growing up in the developing world than there are in the developed world, the primacy of the views of North American and European writers is easy to criticise.

The changing representations of children

The early Renaissance painter, Caravaggio, scoured the streets of Italian towns and cities, sketching the faces and postures of people he encountered. In his paintings, almost always of religious subjects and themes, the faces – smiling, weeping, anguished, joyous – of the people he had sketched appear as Salome or Jesus or Herod. Through the use of line and colour and light he was able to represent anger, disbelief, awe, horror, fear, love – every possible emotion. And the bodies of the people in his paintings are clearly human, capable of movement and repose. His skills were unequalled. And yet, when it came to drawing infants or babies – most often cherubs – this eye for detail and truth and reality seemed to desert him. The babies are unlike any babies you will see anywhere. They are, in proportion and expression, miniature adults. The question of why this is so is a fascinating one and it does not take much imagination to realise that this was not because he was unable to draw babies in proportion. Clearly, this most exceptional of painters could reproduce anything he had seen. It seems likely that the reproduction of babies in his work relates more clearly to the concepts he held of infants. It is tempting to conclude that at that time and throughout much of Europe infants were seen as miniature versions of adults – as adults in waiting. And indeed an analysis of medieval European paintings does seem to suggest as much.

By contrast, during Victorian times the perceived and romanticised innocence of childhood was very evident in images of children. It is interesting to situate this view in the context of growing industrialisation and the development of new capitalist endeavours. Children were depicted in pastel colours, prettified, with softened edges and these images were later transposed to be used in advertising. An example is John Millais' painting, *Bubbles* (1886), which was later used to sell Pears soap and is an image some of you may be familiar with.

What seems evident is that images of childhood have changed over time and do change with place. This means that the conceptions people have of childhood will relate not only to childhood itself but also to attitudes to children, to their positions in the family and society, to how they learn and develop morally, intellectually and emotionally, and to what their rights are.

It was the work of the author Philippe Aries which first drew attention to how notions of children and childhood have changed over time. In his seminal work *Centuries of Childhood* (1962) he suggested that the concept of childhood was a new one that did not exist in medieval time. He studied medieval icons and used them to show how images of Jesus as an infant always showed him as a shrunken adult and linked that to the concept of the homunculus (little man). He went on to argue that, beyond infancy where the child was seen as totally dependent, there was no concept of a child per se and consequently no real concept of childhood as a specific phase of life. He believed that the concept of childhood developed slowly in the upper classes in the sixteenth and seventeenth centuries and only appeared fully in society in the twentieth century. In his argument young people between the ages of seven and fifteen were regarded as adults: they were required to work as apprentices in the fields and later in the factories and entered into what we might regard as adult life at very young ages. The great painters of the Renaissance did not paint realistic infants because they lacked skill but because they perceived of babies as adults in waiting.

Aries went on to examine how the developing concept of the child and of childhood changed the position of young people in society. He argued that with the concept of childhood came a theory of the innocence of the child. Children were to be protected from the dreadful realities of life – from birth and death, sex and world events. Where children had once been merely apprentice adults, age itself was of no consequence, but with the development of childhood as a concept children were increasingly segregated by age. Along with the concept of the child and of childhood came thoughts about leisure and play and work and family roles.

For Aries the changes that came about between the fifteenth and seventeenth centuries could be ascribed to three factors. First there was a change to what was happening within families as children became perceived of as more vulnerable and more valued and in need of protection. Then, at a later stage, children were seen as being in need of discipline and training. Third, with the development of schooling, children's ages were seen as significant and schools were seen as the institutions where children belonged. These changes gradually spread from the upper and middle classes until they affected all classes.

Aries's arguments have been challenged by various authors including Shulamith Shahar (1990) who, in her study of childhood in the Middle Ages concluded that some thinkers did conceive of childhood as being made up of several separate stages. She criticised Aries for using very limited sources (things like the diaries and letters and pictures from primarily French aristocratic homes) in order to describe childhood per se. Her point was that the majority of children were not written about and this is a theme of much of the work that followed.

Later historians, including Heywood (2001), have shown how modern concepts of childhood arose through the different discourses and practices relating to child labour, to criminality and to welfare. The development is sometimes summed up as the path from the child as miniature adult, to the child as sinner, to the child as property, to the school child.

British childhood over time: an illustration

We are talking about childhood as a social construct – which means that the ideas of what childhood is and what children are like are created by adults. It requires little extrapolation from this to see that the adults who construct images of childhood do so within a specific time and place, responding to the economic, political, religious, class and political influences and challenges in place. We will use evidence of how views of childhood and children changed over time within Britain over the past two centuries.

It was in the eighteenth century that a public debate began about children and how they should be thought of, nurtured, disciplined and educated. There were two competing strands operating. At one extreme were the harsh views of John Wesley, the Methodist leader, who urged parents to break the will of the child so that it could be subject to the will of God, and at the other extreme the views of Rousseau and his followers. In his famous and influential book, *Emile* (1762), Rousseau writes of the child as being imbued with goodness – the natural child. He urged teachers and parents to treat the child like a child – which was revolutionary in the sense that although the child was seen as being prepared for adulthood, childhood was given some status as a phase in its own right.

The notion of the natural child evolved into the notion of the romantic child as the Romantic poets Blake, Coleridge and Wordsworth began to explore the essence of the being, the development of self. Although there were variations in the details of how these poets conceived of this, essentially childhood was a state of innocence and a model of what would, inevitably, be lost during later life. The childhoods being reflected here bear little relation to the reality of life for the majority of children in Britain at the time, reflecting the extremely precious and sentimentalised childhoods of the rich. For the poor children, harsher views grew up around the impact of industrialisation, the effect of the French Revolution and the growth of capitalism. The effect of this on the lives of children included a focus on original sin, and parents were urged to teach their children that they were evil. The *Evangelical Magazine* in 1799 referred to children as being 'sinful polluted creatures'. The founder of the Sunday School movement, a woman called Hannah More, carried this even further, believing that children brought into the world a 'corrupt nature and evil disposition' (cited in Hendrick, 1997). Despite these negative views of children, More had an abiding belief in the importance of educating and rearing children.

As the eighteenth century drew to a close, child labour predominated. However, this began to change as factory children and chimney sweeps and apprentices in the cotton mills began to be seen as slaves being denied their childhood. It was then that a new construction of childhood began to be apparent and that the use of children as free labourers died out. The notion of childhood as a specific time and phase characterised by a concern for the welfare and protection of children began to grow. A concern emerged for the safety of children in work, for their weakness as compared with adult workers. In an attempt to define what qualities children had, a definition of the span of childhood was made and in 1883 a Royal Commission declared that childhood ended at age thirteen.

Although all of this was concerned with the universality of childhood, there were clear perceptions that the childhoods of the rich and the poor still varied widely and much attention was paid to the so-called 'delinquent' child. Out of this grew the great education reforms which resulted in compulsory schooling. By the mid-19th century the concerns were mainly on establishing norms and images and it was then that the role of the state in determining aspects of childhood was fixed.

The portrayal of children

When we talk about 'representations' here we are thinking of representation in its cultural sense, and about the socially available images and concepts through which children are thought about and portrayed by others. Images of children in paintings reveal quite clearly how the concept of childhood in the Western world changed and developed. Higonnet (1998) describes how the depiction of children in paintings moved on from the sentimentalised and romanticised representations of painters like Millais and Gainsborough. These were idealised images of children – children without class or gender or culture. You will still find images like these on calendars and birthday cards, on biscuit tins and on adverts that seek to represent children as part of happy families living uncomplicated lives of innocence. Higonnet believes that childhood may be defined largely by what it is not – i.e. it is not adulthood. So childhood itself is portrayed as being 'not adulthood' and therefore without difficulties or problems.

Towards the end of the twentieth century, however, these images were being challenged for their perceived sexual preoccupation. Parents became nervous of photographing or painting their own children naked. You may have read of a case in the United States where the director of an arts centre was charged with promoting obscenity after staging a photographic exhibition by the controversial artist Robert Mablethorpe. (The director was later released.)

If you take the time to examine current images of children you will see a different view of childhood. Children from different cultures and classes, ethnic groups and genders are presented. Sometimes these children are shown as victims but this is certainly not always so. What some theorists believe is happening here is that a new image of childhood is being promoted. Christensen (1999) believes that this new image of childhood is one in which aspects of power relationships between adults and children are played with and where children are often portrayed as the strong, the able, the competent as compared to the weak, embarrassing adults. This is depicted in some of the jokey cartoons or in recent films showing 'adult' babies and infantile adults. This fictional reversal of rules and of roles is almost always temporary, with power ultimately restored to its 'proper' place – i.e. with the adults.

In China at the time of Confucius there was no such thing as a children's playground. Children from wealthy families were looked after by wet-nurses and taught by private tutors. They were constrained by the regulations and formalities of high society at the time. In paintings of children from the Song court we see these well-bred children having time for entertaining themselves. By contrast (and as in many societies) the children of the peasants grew up in the fields and did not go to school. They were alongside their parents, and their areas of play were the places of work for their parents. Illustrations from traditional agricultural manuals show children playing alongside their working parents. An example cited by Bai (2005) shows women working in a room where silkworms are breeding while two young children play with silkworms in a basket.

Moving away from popular images, the images of children in paintings also reflect a changed view of childhood. Paula Rego, born in Portugal and still painting, includes in her work disturbing images of children and of women. The images are drawn from her own experiences, often of poverty and cruelty and imbued with her strong political sensitivities. In 1992 she was invited by the Folio Society to produce a new illustrated version of J. M. Barrie's *Peter Pan*. The pictures reveal images of both Peter and Wendy who are shown in a relationship imbued with sexuality. The young people are neither innocent nor depraved. They are adolescents in the grip of development. The images are disturbing perhaps because they show aspects of the lives of children that many painters have been reluctant to depict. But the realities of the lives of children often include things that are deeply disturbing.

The ways in which children are portrayed in literature and on film give further illustration of the prevailing philosophies of children and childhood. We are all familiar with how children – particularly poor boys – are portrayed in the Victorian novels of Charles Dickens. One such boy, Oliver Twist, is to be both admired and feared: a poor boy subject to tremendous trials but overcoming adversity through his own 'pluckiness'. In France, Gavroche in Victor Hugo's *Les Miserables* is represented in a similar way. In North America Mark Twain gave us a picture of a street child, Huckleberry Finn: a free spirit representing, according to Twain, all that should be avoided for mothers and all that should be aimed at for boys.

Moving into the early twentieth century, representations of the lives of children change. In literature, in art and later in film and cartoon, we find representations of children who did not fit into the conventional mode of Western childhoods – e.g. not only those who were poor heroes but also those living on the streets, being without a family, involved in adult work. Jorge Amado's heroic street child in Brazil was Pedro Bala, in his book *Capitaes de Areia*. This was paralleled in some of the films that were produced particularly in Europe after 1945. In Hollywood the depictions of children in film remained largely sentimentalised and offered a somewhat saccharine version of childhood: by dramatic contrast films produced in post-war Italy moved to revealing the brutal realities of the lives of children. Basil Davidson, writing in the *New Statesman* in 1951, drew attention to how determined Italian film-makers were to depict the reality of life for many in Italian cities and in the countryside. A milestone in cinema depictions of children was *The Bicycle Thieves,* which showed the impact on one child of massive unemployment, the effects of deep poverty and utter despair. From India, too, came films about childhood showing the effects of poverty and deprivation – like Satyajit Ray's famous trilogy.

Along with changing representations of childhood came changes to the language used to discuss children and childhoods and a developing understanding of children's interests and preoccupations. Bai (2005) tells us that in classical China there were no words to describe children's playthings. It was only when Froebel's ideas about play in education were introduced into China at the beginning of the twentieth century that the Chinese invented a word to describe the 'gifts' given to the children of the affluent to play with. In the fields, however, children picked up the things around them and used them to their own purposes. These were their playthings or toys. At the same time some adults were designing things for children to play with and as in Western society today these were often miniatures of things in the adult world. As there were changes from rite to popular customs, children's games developed and these were often incorporated into traditional celebrations. Toy lanterns are a case in point.

In the famous nursery schools of Reggio Emilia, the ways in which language is used reveal their very particular view of children and of childhood. The word 'play' (*giocare* in Italian) is used but less than words like 'culture' and 'competent' and 'challenging' and 'critical'. Learning includes being able to make and challenge meaning, to construct metaphors and explore paradoxes, and to develop and use individual symbols and codes in the process of learning to decode the established symbols and codes of their culture and society. The educators in Reggio Emilia are clear that childhood is a value-laden construct and Rinaldi (2006) explains how political the concept is as she tells us that 'childhood does not exist, we create it as a society, as a public subject. It is a social, political and historic construction' (Rinaldi 2006: 13). This relates closely to the work of Foucault, who looked at how knowledge and power are intertwined in the dominant discourses. In Western culture the dominant discourse when we think about the child includes things like child development and play, and stages of development. These concepts then contribute to how we think about the child – the whole thing being cyclical. Knowledge and power legitimise one another.

Western concepts of childhood

The way in which childhood is perceived in the developed world today is as a very distinct and separate phase of development from adulthood. The very study of child development and, in particular, of those theorists whose work we will examine later in this book and who described childhood as being a linear process of moving from dependence to independence, from immature thought to rational thought, encouraged the growth of this concept of childhood. In much of the developed world childhood itself is now separated out into different phases – early childhood, childhood and adolescence, for example. For each phase there are ideas about what children should and should not be doing, how they should and should not behave and what their world should be like. For this minority group childhood is perceived of as a time of exploration of the world, moving towards adulthood, protected by the family and the state and free from the pressures of economic demands and work.

Powerful in the development of childhood as a unique phase are the advertisers, the manufacturers and the producers of things designed and made specifically for children. Cross (2004), in his analysis of the underpinning philosophy for the development of children as consumers, describes it as 'wondrous innocence'. He argues that the roots of this lie in the romantic view of childhood expressed in the nineteenth century and in the changing views of the middle classes in the US and also in Europe. This view of childhood does not mesh well with the views of educators or psychologists; nonetheless its influence is pervasive and powerful.

Cross analyses the development as having started in the first three decades of the twentieth century, with the growth of magazines for middle-class women. These magazines reached millions of readers and promoted the notion of the child as central to the life and happiness of the adults. The image of the child they promoted was that of the individual, sheltered and scientifically raised child. Adverts consequently promised children (and their parents) brighter, happier, more fulfilled futures if they bought the product. So buying the correct soap could protect the child from illness; ensuring the child had access to a particular toy would ensure future opportunities; buying an insurance policy would guarantee against future hardship, and so on. So the child emerged as an independent being with needs different from those of the parents.

As advertising took hold and a market of specialised goods flourished, so adverts appeared encouraging children to 'teach' their parents. Towards the middle of the century, adverts often featured father–son bonding as a theme for buying. Fathers, like their sons, would enjoy electric train sets, for example. Girls were often featured as prospective users of beauty products and shown with their mothers in female bonding activities around their appearances. Over the twentieth century, Western childhoods came to be treated as imitations of adulthood with children being overwhelmed by miniature versions of 'real' life. No longer was it enough for children to play with sticks and lengths of fabric and empty boxes and sand and water: children were offered miniature ironing boards, guns, tables and chairs, washing machines, and so on. Children's clothes increasingly began to resemble the clothes being worn by their parents and children's fashion became an enormous growth industry. Younger and younger children were encouraged to dress glamorously or casually but in the fashion of the day: to acquire jewellery and use facial products; to consider their nails and have more than one pair of shoes; to explore fantasy worlds through electronic toys. In schools and other settings for young children the wider range of bought equipment the better the education children would receive. That was the implied message and often this was linked to the messages being drawn through the media about what current research into brain activity indicated. Children need to be stimulated and the more varied the stimuli the better the learning. This is something that we challenge throughout this book.

You will recall that we looked briefly at the image of childhood held by educators in Reggio Emilia. For them, the image of a child is, above all, a cultural – and hence a social and political – construct that allows those who hold that image to recognise or ignore some qualities and potentials in children and from that to develop expectations and contexts that will develop the potentials or negate them. Rinaldi says 'What we believe about children thus becomes a determining factor in defining their social and ethical identity, their rights and the educational contexts offered them' (2006: 83). This is something to be considered when reading what follows.

Representations of global childhoods

Many in the developing world find the images of childhood in the developing world deeply offensive. You will be used to images of children as victims – of war, of ethnic cleansing, of poverty, of disease, of natural disasters, of work and of cruelty. The intention behind these images is ostensibly to make an emotional appeal to the rich. In 2005 there was a celebration of Africa across the media. Images of the poor and deprived dominated and Africa was treated as a single entity and its people as suffering and stereotyped. It is important to remember, however, that in doing this these images reinforce the centuries-old creation of the superiority of the developed over the developing world.

In many developed countries, including the UK and the US, there are rich as well as poor children. In these countries the gap between rich and poor is vast and it could be argued that the concept of childhood in these countries is a privilege of the rich and practically non-existent for the poor. This was the finding of Goldstein (1998) who explained that rich children in Brazil share many of the experiences of children in the developed world. They go to school and if they are involved in paid labour this is to a limited extent. Poor children in Brazil are required to contribute to the economy of the family and cannot go to school – except for some who may attend sporadically and infrequently. Some are cut loose from their families and have to live on the streets. Think, too, of the millions of children in sub-Saharan Africa who, as a result of the Aids pandemic, are themselves heads of families. But can we say that for these children childhood does not exist? Clearly there are aspects of their lives that are terrible and urgently need to be improved, but if we deny them the existence of a childhood we characterise childhood as the domain of the rich. Prout (2005) suggests that we need to broaden our concept of childhood to include the childhoods of the poor as well as those of the rich. In other words childhood itself cannot be seen as a single simple concept but one that has to take on the diversity of the reality of childhoods across the world.

Rosemberg (2005) adds another dimension to the argument. In her study of childhood and inequality in Brazil she points to the dominance of presenting what is problematic – being poor, being black, being indigenous, being 'the other' – and asks why there is no focus on what it means to be white, to be of European origins, to speak the dominant language. Very rarely do we question how the dominant status of one group is maintained over generations. That would require us to examine what it is we have to do to maintain our position vis-á-vis the rest of the world. Rosemberg notes that many recent developments (increased urbanisation, access to television, falling infant mortality and fertility rates, for example) are contributing to the concept of childhood in Brazil. Parents are reconsidering their patterns of child-rearing. They see young children as intelligent. The role of the father is being reconceptualised.

Pawan Gupta (2005) examined concepts of childhood in mountain villages in the Himalayas. She found that the mountain communities were, on the whole, functioning well and that the impact of modernity on them was not helping them move forward as anticipated but rather making these traditional societies more fractured. The result, she tells us, is that the communities are losing confidence in their own abilities, their own styles of child-rearing, their own value systems. Her advice is that the space of traditional societies must be restored so that their confidence is regained and they can take their own initiatives.

Helen Penn (2005) spent some time in Kazakhstan and highlighted the advantages to children of living in the old Soviet system. Children had freedom and mobility, showed respect for their elders, were part of extended families where child-rearing was shared. Children were thought of as valuable to society – principles upheld by both Soviet society and Central Asian nomadic culture. With the breakdown of the Soviet Union the kindergartens for children, the health services and the water and sanitation facilities broke down. Alongside this has come the impoverishment of women and children – not only in Kazakhstan but also in many of the countries that were part of the Soviet Union. In the first five years after transition the amount of GDP spent on social security decreased by about 90 per cent, and education and health spending by more than 50 per cent. Families are unable to protect children from the negative outcomes associated with this, despite the traditional pride families take in children.

Images of childhood and poverty

One of the most significant and neglected factors in discussions of child development is that of poverty. The United Nation's Children's Fund (UNICEF) stated that 90 per cent of the world's wealth was owned by only 10 per cent of the world's population (UNICEF 2000). It appears that the poor of the world are getting poorer and many believe that this is caused by the impact of the International Monetary Fund and the World Bank imposing a free-market economy on the economies of Africa, Asia and South America. What this means is a cut in state expenditure on vital issues like health, welfare and education, reversing state ownerships of various bodies, and removing or lowering barriers to free trade. For some countries these measures have been effective, but for many they have resulted in debt and retrenchment. Prout (2005) tells us that

> Between 1998 and 1993 the real income of the world's poorest five per cent actually fell by over a quarter (UNICEF, 1996). In 1990 the annual income per person in high-income countries was 56 times greater than in low-income countries: by 1999 it was 63 times greater (UNICEF, 2001). The number of people struggling to survive on less than $1 per day (the international measure of absolute poverty) rose by ten million for every year of the 1990s.
>
> (Prout 2005: 18)

The ways in which poverty itself is depicted and the effect that poverty has on the lives of children and families are worthy of attention. For the millions of children across the developing world, living without clean water, sanitation, health care or enough food, life is difficult. Parents often struggle to know how to deal with the problems they face. Often these parents are characterised as inadequate or uncaring, when, in reality, they are merely overwhelmed by what life has dealt them. Descriptions of the lives of such families abound: Nancy Scheper-Hughes (1993) writes of the neglect and resulting high infant mortality rate in the *favelas* of Northeast Brazil, and Phillipe Bourgois (1998) of similar issues in the *barrios* of New York where he worked with Puerto Rican families.

But poverty is also an issue in the developed world, and economic policies are ensuring that the divides between rich and poor in the US and Europe are still increasing. This was recently and poignantly illustrated by the impact of hurricane Katrina on the American South where the poorest and most traumatised people were primarily black, old, women and children. In various developed countries the existence of some sort of welfare state provides a degree of protection from the more heinous effects of poverty. Nonetheless, the differences between the most affluent and the poorest continue to increase and there has been a particular impact on children. In a recent OECD study (Oxley et al., 2000) of 17 developed countries, 12 showed a growing inequality between the children of rich and poor.

Penn (2005) argues that even within the poorest groups there are things that are positive about poverty. She points to the findings of Majid Rahnema (1997) who found that within poor communities life was not meaningless, but grounded in a valuable non-consumerist way of living. There may be some truth in this, although critics find it a somewhat romanticised view of poverty.

Representations of children: children as players

We have seen how childhood has been an intensively regulated phase of life with decisions about the lives of children made almost entirely by adults. It was only towards the end of the twentieth century that the view of children as social beings – as players in their own life stories – began to be accepted as a principle. This was evidenced by the rights of children being encoded in Article 12 of the UN Convention on the Rights of the Child, which states:

> States Parties shall assure to the child who is capable of forming his or her own views the right to express those views freely in all matters affecting the child, the views of the child being given due weight in accordance with the age and maturity of the child.
>
> For this purpose, the child shall in particular be provided the opportunity to be heard in any judicial and administrative proceedings affecting the child, either directly, or through a representative or an appropriate body, in a manner consistent with the procedural rules of national law.

Mayall *et al.* (1996) have looked at children's views on health and worked with them in schools, treating them as social actors. Children are a minority group in the sense that they lack power to influence their own lives. They may well have views and even be able to articulate these and be heard, but the decisions to be made remain remote from them. There are a range of constraints which stop them from being full participants. What Mayall *et al.* do is to link the sociological study of children in schools to a political agenda which goes beyond the notion of rights.

Some slow progress is being made in the area of children as actors, as people begin to reflect on how the previously dualistic versions of childhood (for example, as a time of innocence versus as a time of evil) made it difficult for children to be perceived of as anything other than dependent. However, now, in countries throughout the world, children are becoming social actors for justice. Some of the examples of this come from South Asia where 45 per cent of the population lives below the income required to meet minimum daily needs and where the disparities between rich and poor are becoming some of the widest in the world (Haq 2000). Children are beginning to ask out loud questions about fairness and justice. How fair and just a society is believed to be is determined by who has the power and how it is used. Social justice implies justice for the poor, the marginalised, the exploited, the oppressed and the denied. Redistribution of wealth goes some way towards addressing these inequalities, but the notion of rights is important too. Children are emerging from their invisibility as both active citizens and social actors.

Raman (2000) points out that understanding the concept of childhood cannot be separated from understanding the wider context:

> The very definition of the selfhood, subjecthood and personhood is deeply scripted by the larger context. The impact of macro-structures and processes operating at a wider societal level affect groups differentially determining the life-choices of groups and individuals.
>
> (Raman 2000: 12)

O'Kane (2002) uses this to analyse how concepts of childhood have changed in South Asia. Culturally, children in South Asia were not encouraged to express their views or to take part in decision-making processes at any level. Children, she says, were seen as the property of their parents. Through the development of some children's collective organisations like the Bal Mazdoor Union (a union of child workers in Delhi) and Bhima Sangha (a union of working children in South India), both of which have been in existence for more than a decade, children have found a voice to express concerns about grave events. A case in point was the death of fifteen-year-old worker Zaffar Imam, killed by his employer in 1994, the deaths of three street children at the Government Observation Home at Delhi Gate also in 1994, and the brutal killings of Gond tribal women and children in Nagpur. All of these cases were discussed by the children and this discussion has been documented (Reddy 2000; White 2001) The impact of this on the views of parents and the community is worth considering. How will views of childhood change over the coming decades? Theis (2001) suggests that there is an ongoing paradigm shift in relation to children and to childhoods. Changes at many levels will results from this – changes to theory and practice, attitudes and language, laws and rights.

Craig (2003) offers us some interesting case studies of projects aimed at involving children and young people working on sensitive issues including racism. One of these relates to work being done in Germany involving Turkish mothers and children, and McIvor (1995) has reported on a project where disabled children in Morocco are challenging their dependent status and critically examining how they are both portrayed and viewed by others. People involved in immigration work in the UK are beginning to be aware of the silence of those children and young adults living in situations of great uncertainty and this is surely a field worth researching.

Becoming a good parent

Much has been said and written about the importance of parents in considerations of how children learn and develop. We do not have space here to explore patterns of child-rearing and parenting across time and cultures, but we do have time to consider how images of 'parenting' affect how we conceive of children and their development. We have seen how dominant Western views of child development have been, and discussed how much of the work has been done with white middle-class children and their families. Underpinning much of the work has been the assumption that 'everybaby' lives in a home with two parents: a mother and a father. We know that this idealised family is reality for the minority of the world's children and we have seen how poverty and disease impact on family structures.

Along with this has been the widely held view that the role of parents – particularly of mothers – is crucial in deciding the success of children. Intervention programmes, developed in response to the idea that poor children need the rich to intervene to provide more stimulation for the children (not to address poverty and inequality per se) and offer advice to parents such as 'Speak to your children; read to them; use English with them; play games with them'. Lamb (1999) suggests that what is conveyed through the psychological literature about parenting includes the following:

- Children need to have two parents – one of each gender.
- Parents should divide up family responsibilities between them with the mothers being home-makers, care takers and child-rearers (because they are better suited to these roles) and the fathers earning the living.
- Young children should be cared for primarily within the family and by family members.
- White middle-class parents have superior parenting skills and thus have children who are more likely to excel.

You will know that even within the developed North this model of the idealised family is uncommon. Hochschild (2001) wrote about the care chain in America where middle-class American mothers employed women immigrants from the South to care for their children while the children of these migrant workers were left behind. We find this pattern here in the UK today, where many Eastern European women have come here to work in order to earn more money to support the children they have left behind. This pattern of well-to-do people depending for the care of their children on the poor, at the expense of the carers' own children, is documented across time and place.

Currently in the UK there are many projects designed to 'teach' parents how to 'parent'. This is clearly based on some image of 'the good parent' and this, by definition, is a monocultural, oversimplifed and Western model.

An image for the twenty-first century?

We have looked, briefly, at how the concepts of childhood and children change over time, place and circumstance. We have seen that how children are represented sometimes gives an indication of how they are perceived within a culture or group, remembering always that often only certain children are represented in literature or art or film. We have considered the pervasiveness of Western ideas in many discussions about children and their development and have seen how vital aspects like poverty are ignored or discussed in pejorative ways, suggesting that simple solutions can solve the immense problems created.

We need an image of the child to work with for the purposes of this book. The image suggested by Loris Malaguzzi offers a meaning-making child, situated in a culture, coming from a rich history and being enabled to make meaning, represent feelings and ideas, and challenge existing structures. The image we hold of the child is, as we have said, one of the factors that will determine how we conceive of development. Here is our twenty-first-century child drawn on the model suggested by Rinaldi (2006).

From birth she is engaged in building a relationship with the world and intent on experiencing it so that she develops a complex system of abilities, strategies for learning and ways of organising relationship. So she is able to make her own personal maps for her own development and orientation – social, cognitive, emotional and symbolic. She is making meaning from events from very early on and she will share her meanings through representations and language. She will make and take and share meanings through stories. She is a competent and active and critical child – thus one who might be described by the word challenging. Challenging is often used as a negative term but we use it to suggest that the child is challenging because she can produce change and movement in the various systems with which she is involved. These include the family, the setting, the school, the society. She is a player in her society. The child makes culture, values and rights and is competent in learning and in living. This child can explore a range of realities, can construct metaphors, seeing what is like what and why that matters. She can make and explore paradoxes, seeing what is different and why that matters. She can invent symbols and codes and use these to help her learn to decode the conventional means of symbolisation prevalent in her culture and community. Living within a community she will learn from all those around her through interaction, watching, listening, being an apprentice and being a teacher.

Questions

- What do you now understand about why both history and culture are important to an understanding of child development?
- What importance does a view of childhood as a separate and distinct phase have in terms of understanding global development and where do things like poverty and rights fit into this?
- What have you learned about how dominance continues over generations and about the effect of this dominance on the confidence of those in the developing world with regard to their customs, approaches, traditions and cultures?

Chapter 2

The child as meaning maker

In this chapter we start to investigate the field of child development, which is often described as being a scientific exploration of how children learn and develop. In doing this we examine the work of Jean Piaget, one of the key theorists in the field of child development, and examine what he said about how the human infant, from birth onwards, begins to make meaning in order to understand the world and the objects in it. Piaget had a tremendous impact on our understanding but his work has been criticised on a number of grounds and we also look at his critics.

> In a restaurant a small child and her older sister are each given a balloon attached to a long shiny thread. The older child is interested in the balloon and stares intently at it, watching how it moves when she pulls the string. The younger child immediately puts the thread in her mouth and uses her tongue and her lips to explore it. What questions can she be asking as she does this? She is clearly using her tongue and lips which are very sensitive to get a feeling of the sleekness of the thread. It is only by chance that she notices the balloon attached to her thread when her sister laughs when the two balloons collide. The look of amazement on her face is wonderful.

From conception to birth

It takes about 40 weeks from conception to birth. For nine months the human infant inhabits its first environment. Housed in the mother's watery womb the foetus develops as cells divide and multiply, becoming organs –the eyes, the ears, the heart and lungs, the brain and pancreas, the stomach and bowels – until the human foetus is ready to live independently and outside of the womb. Born into a world of light and noise and smell and sensation the infant starts to demonstrate an extraordinary capacity to learn and develop from the moment of birth. Indeed, there are some theorists who suggest that there is evidence of learning even before birth.

Although it is dark in the womb there is evidence that if a bright light is shone on the foetus in the womb three months before birth, the foetus responds by making a sudden movement. This suggests that the foetus is able to use sight to detect a change in the light in the womb. Similarly, if a heavy object is placed on the womb the foetus tends to push against it with some part of his or her own body. This suggests that the foetus is able to both detect and respond to pressure. The womb is not a silent place; the foetus is able to hear the sounds of the mother's heart beat and the rumble of the amniotic fluid and – some theorists suggest – the sound of voices. From the response of infants to the sound of their mother's voice immediately after birth there is evidence that before birth the foetus is able to tune in to the pitch and intonation patterns of the mother's voice (Karmiloff-Smith 1994).

After nine months of sharing the mother's physiology, the baby releases hormones into the mother's bloodstream and it is this that triggers labour. Birth itself is regarded by many as traumatic and there is evidence that immediately after birth the infant is more alert and awake than she or he will be for some time to come. The reason for this is that the infant's adrenaline levels have soared to enable the baby to cope with the traumatic changes from the relative quiet and gloom of the womb, through the birth canal and into the unfamiliar, bright and noisy world. It is now in the developed world that certain medical tests are carried out on infants. These tests are aimed to check that the baby is responding appropriately to a range of stimuli.

The child as empty vessel?

In the first chapter we looked at how views of children and of childhood change over time and place. The human infant, born anywhere in the world from Africa to North America and beyond, actively seeks to discover and understand the world which he or she inhabits. We are so accustomed to thinking about human infants as active learners that we struggle to understand how they could, for so many years, have been viewed as no more than blank slates or empty vessels.

One of the earliest thinkers in the field of child development was Burrhus Skinner. He was an American psychologist who became interested in behaviourism – a theory which emphasised the importance of the external world on development. He was interested in what could be seen and heard and tested, and not interested in things like feelings or motives or intentions. In other words his focus was on the observable aspects of behaviour at the expense of the hidden internal processes. For him, a child was the sum total of their genetic inheritance, their past history and their current situation. In summary, he believed that responses to an action can either increase the likelihood of that action being repeated or decrease the likelihood. An action that is regarded as desirable (like saying thank you) can be reinforced by the child being given a reward – a kiss or a smile or a sweet, for example. This positive reinforcement, repeated again and again, is what helps the child learn that saying thank you is a good thing to do. Swearing, on the other hand, might be negatively reinforced by a reprimand, being sent to bed without supper or even being smacked. The child learns that swearing should not be repeated. It is a model of learning and development which depends on the child doing something and the response from the adult determining whether what the child did is rewarded or not. Those familiar with the work of Pavlov will recognise this model of learning: Pavlov used the term *operant conditioning* to describe it. The organism (in the case of Skinner the child) does something (the stimulus) and the adult involved responds (the response). This stimulus–response model is both simple and crude and cannot account for the subtle and complex aspects of learning.

The child as active learner?

Jean Piaget was the first Western theorist to consider the infant as more than a blank slate waiting to be written on. By training as a biologist, he used his investigations of how organisms adapt to the environment to inform the studies he made of children's cognitive development and thinking. Through acute observations of his own children he concluded that the human infant was actively seeking to make sense. He noted that the human infant is born with the ability to adapt to and learn from the environment. Essentially, then, learning is the result of interaction between the child and the environment. Through this the child takes information from the environment and uses this to change what Piaget called 'mental structures'. Thus cognitive development took place through three processes which he called *accommodation, assimilation* and *equilibrium.* The language he used makes his theories seem daunting, but with some unpicking they become more accessible.

Assimilation can be thought of as follows:

- the infant takes in or assimilates every new experience or event and adds this to an existing and ever-growing store of memories and/or understandings;
- through these repeated additions the infant is later able to classify and order experiences and meaning.

Accommodation can be thought of as follows:

- sometimes an experience or event challenges some earlier understanding and when this happens some mental adjustment has to be made;
- something about a new experience may mean that the child has to accommodate an earlier understanding in order to adapt to the environment.

For Piaget, accommodation was a higher-order cognitive process than assimilation and he saw it as the process that allows human beings to become the effective problem-solvers they so patently are. Piaget believed that the goal of every child, every learner, was cognitive equilibrium. It is important to consider that cognitive equilibrium or balance can only ever be partially achieved as a stepping stone to more adequate forms of knowing. Piaget used the phrase 'active learner' to indicate his theory that the human infant is never passive in the learning process but is mentally or cognitively active and pro-active in seeking to make sense of the world. Meadows (1993) gives an amusing example to help readers understand the difficult concepts of assimilation and accommodation. She adds another dimension which she calls organisation.

Her example relates to an experienced cook who has successfully cooked carrots and potatoes. She has boiled, roasted, fried and mashed potatoes and made them into chips. She has boiled carrots, grated them for salad and made them into soup. So she has used a range of methods for successfully preparing these two vegetables.

A matrix can be drawn up as shown on the next page (note that x indicates a successful attempt).

The cook is then introduced to parsnips for the first time. She is able to assimilate parsnips into the carrot category, because she feels they are similar in shape and texture. She is able to boil them and make them into a soup – a rather bland soup, it must be said. She grates them for a salad but they look unattractive. She is also able to assimilate them into her potato category. They mash well, can be chipped or fried and are, says Meadows, delicious roasted.

A second matrix then is given.

Matrix 1   Carrots and potatoes

Method	Carrots	Potatoes
Boiling	x	x
Chipping	Not tried	x
Frying	Not tried	x
Grating, for salad	x	Not tried
Mashing	Not tried	x
Roasting	Not tried	x
Soup	x	Not tried

(Meadows 1993: 199)

Matrix 2   Carrots, potatoes and parsnips

Method	Parsnips
Boiling	x
Chipping	Possible
Frying	Possible
Grating, for salad	Maybe
Mashing	x
Roasting	x
Soup	Maybe

(Meadows 1993: 200)

Meadows goes on to add that assimilation is always accompanied by accommodation. So the schema of what we might call 'mashable vegetables' now consists not only of potatoes but also includes parsnips and with repeated experience of root vegetables (with the possible addition of butter) can be extended eventually to include carrots, Jerusalem artichokes and so on.

Some examples related to a child may illustrate these concepts and make their meaning more apparent:

Thandi has had experience of drinking milk from her bottle and does so with ease. We could say that she is a skilled bottle-drinker. She can grasp and lift the bottle, put it to her lips and drink from it. When her carer puts a new bottle which is much larger and full of milk in front of her she attempts to assimilate this new object into her schema of grasping and drinking and in doing this she draws on her experience of bottles. But she finds that although she can grasp the bottle she cannot lift it because it is too heavy. The only way in which she can accommodate to this new situation is to seek help and the only way in which she can do this is to cry. Her mother lifts the bottle for her and they hold it together while she drinks.

Eleni has been drinking from a cup for some time now. When an empty cup is placed in front of her she asks for a drink. Her behaviour demonstrates that she responds appropriately and in the same way to a familiar situation and this could be explained as having reached equilibrium.

The concept of equilibrium or equilibration is a complex one and one that many writers find difficult to explain, partly because Piaget's own definitions seemed to change over time, but it does appear to be closely related to the focus in his theory that all cognition is directed to a *logico-mathematical model*. This is another concept that needs exploration and is, at first reading, difficult to understand. Piaget considered a logical operation to be an internalised, mental action, part of a logical system. Logical operations are things like *seriation* (being able to organise things in a logical sequence), *classification* (being able to sort things into categories on some logical basis of similarity or difference, inclusion or exclusion) and *numeration*.

Seriation is said to refer to the understanding of the relationships of position in space and in time. The child explores and comes to understand things like height and length and width. A classic example is when a child demonstrates the ability to work out which stick is longer by using a third stick of intermediate length.

————————————————————	A
—————————————————	C
————————————————	B

The two sticks whose length the child is comparing are sticks A and B. Stick C, which is the stick of intermediate length, is clearly shorter than stick A but longer than stick B. The child compares stick A with stick C and makes some judgement about its length and then compares the intermediate stick C to stick B. What is required is that the child can understand, remember and store what has been found out and then apply these double relationships of C with A and C with B. The child can only do this when he or she has reached the stage of concrete operations.

Classification involves the child in being able to consider things like inclusion and exclusion, and Piaget's famous (or perhaps infamous) example is where children are asked questions about a bead necklace made up of seven brown and three white beads. The children are asked, 'Are there more beads or are there more brown beads?' In Piaget's terminology the superordinate class (the one that includes everything) is that of beads and the subordinate class (the one that is included in the superordinate class) is that of brown beads. Not surprisingly young children find this nonsensical question difficult to answer and mainly respond by saying there are more brown beads. The analysis of this you may well make is that younger children are being extremely rational and logical in giving this response because the question makes little sense. Piaget's explanation is that younger children have not logically recognised the relationship between the set and the subset.

Numeration is a combination of seriation and classification. Young children count objects but Piaget believed that it was only with an understanding of seriation and classification that they could understand numbers as a sequence and then be able to classify them into sets of classes and sub-classes. Much doubt has been thrown on these concepts and the findings Piaget arrived at. They are cited here only to try and explain something about logico-mathematical reasoning.

An important aspect of Piaget's work is often claimed to be that it allowed those studying child development to begin to think about cognitive development as a process. Learning takes place and provides a foundation for future learning. This high-lights clearly how children are actively constructing knowledge about the world. The cognitive structures and processes allow them to actively select what about the input is meaningful to them and then to represent, re-represent and transform what they have selected in accordance with their current understanding. Flavell tells us that it is the 'active nature of their intellectual commerce with the environment (that) makes them to a large degree the manufacturers of their own development' (1992: 998).

A linear approach to development

Piaget, observing how children grow and change over time, saw development as linear and suggested there were four major cognitive stages in the development of logic and thinking. He saw these stages as corresponding to four successive forms of knowledge and believed that during each of these stages children were thinking and reasoning in different ways. For Piaget the stages were age-related, although some writers on Piaget suggest that the ages of attainment he gave were only approximate (Goswami 2001). This is very much open to debate and this aspect of his work has been much criticised. Nonetheless, Piaget's stage theory in particular has influenced many aspects of how children are educated in Britain, in the US and in much of Europe and many people find it difficult to think of learning in a less linear fashion. Piaget's stages are as follows:

1 The sensory-motor period: 0–2 years
2 The period of pre-operations: 2–7 years
3 The period of concrete operations: 7–11 years
4 The period of formal operations: 11–12 years upward.

The sensory-motor phase

In this phase cognition was seen as being based on physical interaction with the world. Piaget saw thought developing from action. It is as though these infant meaning-seek-ers use the means available to them in their earliest development – their senses and their own movements – to try and make sense of every encounter with objects, people and events, asking 'What is this?' and then, perhaps, 'What does it do?' and still later 'What can I do with it?' Anyone familiar with infants will recognise the incessant exploration of the physical world and appreciate Piaget's suggestion that this is not random or hap-hazard, but a construction of meaning. As Goswami puts it, 'sensory-motor behaviours *became* thought' (2001: 260). Central to development in this period is the concept of *object permanence* and it is here, again, that many critics feel unhappy with Piaget's expla-nations. For Piaget, it is only at the age of about 15–18 months that the infant is able to retain the concept of object permanence. This means that the human infant, up to that age, is not able to appreciate that an object or a person, hidden from view, still exists. Piaget suggests that this is because the infant is unable to create and sustain a cognitive representation of the object or person. When the object or person is no longer visible the infant cannot call up a memory or representation of it. For many critics this view is unacceptable, suggesting as it does that true and meaningful cognitive activity is delayed for so long.

Recent research in the US suggests that infants as young as five months of age can make mental images or representations of objects. Luo *et al.* (2003) carried out an experiment on five-month-old infants who were shown a tall cylinder move back and forth behind a low screen. The experimental hypothesis was that the infants would form a prediction based on the experience of seeing two objects and when one or both objects were obscured (or had 'disappeared') the infants would show surprise. This would register as paying attention to the strange event and paying attention usually means watching for a longer period of time.

Piaget's views on the inability of the young child to make mental images were related to the view he held that children in the sensory-motor stage were essentially *egocentric* in their thinking. By egocentric he meant an inability to perceive the world from the perspective of anybody else.

The pre-operational phase

In this phase (between two and seven years of age) Piaget suggested that ideas about the properties and the relationships of concrete objects developed. And it was here that he found evidence of this egocentrism. He saw the child as solving all problems and interpreting the world in terms of the self. For him the child at this stage was essentially unable to use logical thinking and was locked into a subjective understanding of the world.

The concrete operations phase

During the next stage, egocentricity begins to wane; the child begins to be able to *decentre* (or consider multiple aspects of any situation at the same time) and achieves some understanding of *reversibility* (the understanding that any operation or action on an object implies its inverse or its opposite). The development of concrete operational mental structures such as *classification* (grouping things that are the same or similar for some reason), *seriation* (arranging things in some logical sequence or order) and *conservation* (the understanding that despite apparent visible changes some things remain constant or the same) characterise thinking during this stage.

Some of the most vociferous criticisms of Piaget's work relate to the experiments he devised and conducted to assess how well children were able to conserve ideas of number or mass or weight. Conservation, for him, was a key logical concept which underpins the understanding of invariance, and this is essential in understanding things like number systems. Classic experiments required the child to compare two initially identical situations, one of which was later changed in some way. To illustrate this, let us look at the conservation of number. A child was shown two rows of beads arranged in an array demonstrating one-to-one correspondence. While the child watched, the adult rearranged one of the rows of beads, making the spaces between the beads wider so that the arrays were no longer visually identical. Piaget found that most children under the age of about seven said, when asked, that there were more beads in the array where the beads were more widely spaced. Was this an example of an inability to conserve quantity? Or was there something about the test situation itself that suggested to the child that the adult required an answer other than the obvious one? (Remember the child had watched the adult moving the beads!)

Margaret Donaldson (1978) was a stern critic of some of Piaget's ideas and she felt that the test itself was flawed. She and a colleague developed a new test, now known as the 'naughty teddy' test, where the children were told that they were going to play a game and were given a cardboard box which contained a teddy bear. The children were told that the teddy had been very naughty and kept escaping from the box to mess up the toys and spoil the game. Two identical rows of conservation beads (described above) were brought out and the children asked 'Are there more here or more here or are they both the same number?' Then the naughty teddy appeared and began to mess about, moving the beads on one array. The teddy was scolded and the children asked the same question again. Most of the children (even those as young as four) were able to 'conserve'. In a meaningful context, where there was a reason for the beads to have been moved, the children were not fooled by the seemingly nonsensical question asked in the original experiments.

The formal operations phase

This final stage is achieved with the child able to generate hypotheses and think scientifically. One of the most significant aspects of thinking at this stage is reasoning by analogy. This requires the thinker to reason about the similarities between the *relations* of objects. Young children, you will remember, were said not to be able to do this. Here is an example cited by Goswami (2001).

The analogy is '*Bicycle is to handlebars as ship is to* ... ?' (The answer, you will have worked out if you know anything about ships, is 'ship's wheel'.) When Piaget gave a pictorial version of this to young children they gave answers like 'bird' and when questioned found similarities to justify their response. One example quoted by Goswami is of the child giving a perfectly acceptable response of 'ships and birds are both found on the lake'. Piaget's explanation was that children solved analogies on the basis of associations and their inability to solve some of the analogies appears to have related to lack of knowledge. How many young children would have understood that the question related to the way in which bicycles and ships were steered, for example? Goswami and Brown (1989) carried out a series of pictorial item analogies with very young children and based these on the types of relationships young children would have experienced and hence understood. An example of this is '*Chocolate is to melted chocolate as snowman is to* ... ?' Or '*Playdoh is to cut playdoh as apple is to* ... ?' Remember that these were in pictorial form. The finding that children as young as three are able to think analogically is an interesting one.

Much criticism has been made of the linear and age-related stage theory posited by Piaget. Critics feel that although children do develop and change, not all learning is linear and learners often resort to strategies that they have used earlier in life. An example is what adult learners do when they are faced with a new technological gadget. Piaget might have suggested that the experienced learner, operating at the stage of formal operations, might use their prior learning and experience in order to know that the best thing to do might be to read the documents that accompany the new gadget. In effect, often what happens is learners use their movements and senses in order to try and work out what they can do with the new gadget. Piaget, you will remember, believed that the thinking was different at each stage and that a child could only progress to the next stage once the requirements of the previous stage had been met. It is an approach of focusing on what learners cannot yet do.

Schemas: repeated patterns of action

One of the features of exploration Piaget noted was the tendency to repeat patterns of action or behaviour. Piaget used the term *schema* to describe these repeated patterns (although, as Athey (1990) notes, there is some debate over whether there are different meanings for the words 'scheme' and 'schema'). For the purposes of this piece schemas can be described as patterns of actions that can be repeated and that lead to the ability to categorise and then to be logically classified. Early patterns of motor behaviour that are repeatable are things like grasping and shaking of objects, and tracking and gazing at objects; later patterns include things like exploring rotation, verticality, enveloping and so on. Much has been written about schemas and how an understanding of them helps educators to see the purposefulness of children's sometimes seemingly random and haphazard explorations. Athey (ibid.) suggests that the history of a particular schema is important. If early schemas are applied in different contexts and through diverse events, the child will have assimilated a broad range of contents. This, according to Hunt (1961), is how knowledge is acquired. The assumption is that the more the experiences and the more diverse the experiences, the better the learning. This is something we will return to later in this book. An example might make this clearer:

> Abdul grasps whatever is placed in his hand – his mother's finger, a spoon, a toy. This is a reflex response in this new born child. With time and experience, however, this reflex grasp becomes elaborated and Abdul can soon reach out, curling and retracting his fingers. Theorists suggest that as this happens there are changes in brain function as electrochemical pathways in the brain lay down what may be called a mental map of the grasping response. For Abdul what is happening is movement and the sensation of grasping different objects. This enables Abdul to develop a disposition or a desire or a habit to grasp objects and within time Abdul uses the grasp purposefully, in order to hold something and later still Abdul will grasp one object rather than another – making a choice. This is the progression from simple reflex to more complex schema and this is only possible because he has a mental map or a mental representation of the actions.

Making sense of symbols

Important, too, in Piaget's thinking is the whole notion of *symbolic representation* or symbolic functioning. Young children become more and more able to represent symbolically things or events they have experienced. This can be in the form of representational thought – images or ideas which are internal and not accessible to outside view – or can be external in the form of drawings, models, speech or symbolic play. To begin with, children symbolically draw on and represent or re-present (present again) objects or events they have experienced. The educators in the famous nursery schools in the Reggio Emilia region of Italy often talk about the importance of representing and re-representing experiences and ideas. They see this as an essential way in which children can explore ideas and feelings, thoughts and emotions. Piaget, you will remember, retained a focus on the cognitive importance of representation. Representation then means the ability to play over and over again, in the mind, the way things look or feel or the patterns of movement made or felt. The term 'action images' is used by Athey to describe the sort of symbolic representation we all see: the child using a stick to be a gun, the block to be a mobile phone, the bucket to be a hat, and so on.

An example which should make this clearer is provided by Allery (1998), who tracked what Colin (aged two years and seven months) did when playing in the garden of the setting. She noticed him put a football in a mop bucket and use the football as a baby and the mop bucket as a pram. Here is some of what happened:

> Anabel, aged four and a half, came over to Colin.
> 'Can I have the ball, Colin?'
> Colin looked at her. He seemed puzzled. She picked the ball up and kicked it away from her.
> 'Nooo!' Colin cried and ran after the ball ...
> Colin picked up the ball. 'Don't run away, baby. It's all right' he said lovingly. He then put the ball under his arm and pulled the bucket over to a small chair. He sat down on the chair and put the ball in the bucket. 'Going shops in a minute, baby, shops and sweets, baby, yeah?' he said.
>
> (Allery 1998: 30)

Coming to understand how one thing can stand for or represent another is important in view of the fact that much that children encounter will be symbolic. In the developed world and much of the developing world children will encounter signs and symbols and in the same way as they try to make sense of the physical world they will try to make sense of this symbolic world. Most obviously the symbols they will encounter will include the relatively simple-to-decode pictorial symbols, but also numeric symbols, alphabetic symbols and the many signs and symbols that define a culture. Gunther Kress (1997) uses the terms *semiotics, signs* and *symbols* to clarify thinking about this:

- Semiotics is the study of the meaning of systems of signs. (Language is a system of signs and so is clothing.)
- Signs are a combination of meaning and form. (The form of a road sign, for example, is something made of metal and the meaning relates to some information or warning about roads and/or traffic.)
- Symbols encapsulate and convey meaning. (The numeral two means more than one and less than 3; the letters c-a-t in English represent the animal cat; the red cross indicates a place where help for injured or sick can be given.)

You will appreciate from this that the young child, faced with making sense of these systems of signs, is actually confronted with learning how to 'read' the world. This is something else we will return to in later chapters.

From Piaget we have learned that the child is curious and actively trying to understand the objects, people and experiences encountered. Piaget's focus was very much on how knowledge was constructed and his model of the child was close to that of Kant, i.e. the child being born with structures that allow him or her to make sense of the world. So knowledge is constructed through interaction with the environment and developmental change is qualitative and occurs through a series of stages.

Rationality and the child as developing scientist

Cannella and Viruru (2004) argue that Piaget's notion of the importance of equilibration supports the notion of the child as miniature scientist. For Piaget, the child identifies some problem in understanding or interpreting an aspect of the world and tries out some hypotheses in an attempt to resolve the problem. The importance of logical thinking is highlighted and the senses and the emotions are not emphasised (Silin 1995). For Piaget, learning is an individual activity with a focus on concepts. Some writers suggest that this led to vital aspects of learning and exploration to be ignored in favour of the logico-mathematical approaches. Egan (1988) suggests the absence of fantasy, and Tobin (1997) adds to that the absence of pleasure.

Prout and James (1990) state that there are three key themes in Western theories of child development, one of which they call 'rationality'. Being rational means being able to use logical reasoning and hence being able to think mathematically. According to Piaget, the child only reaches this stage of thought in adolescence and the implications of this are that early thinking is irrational and children are apprentice thinkers in terms of rationality until they reach Piaget's stage of formal operations. For many researchers and theorists this approach both represents an oversimplification of rationality and marginalises children's intellectual capacities. There are examples of very young children demonstrating a deep understanding of issues like injustice, war, fear, danger and so on. Bolloten and Spafford give the case study of Saeed, a refugee from the war in Northern Somalia, in a Year 5 class in the UK. Saeed wrote about his experiences as in the example quoted here:

> 'Once me and my mum had to change our names and lie about who we were so we could go in a house and have enough to eat and sleep there for the night. That night we had to be disguised.'
>
> (Rutter and Jones, cited in Bolloten and Spafford 2001: 120)

During the apartheid years in South Africa children were routinely detained, arrested, tortured and even killed. At the Harare Conference many children testified to their horrific experiences. Here is a small part of the testimony of 12-year-old Moses Madia (re-written by a lawyer to whom he recounted his experiences). He describes sharing a cell with his 14-year-old friend Charlie and explains that he was unable to eat because he felt nauseous

> '...and on various occasions dizzy and disoriented. I found it difficult to sleep and consequently I felt very tired with the result that when the nausea occurred I often broke down crying. I have no idea why I was arrested and detained as I have committed no illegal acts, nor been involved in any unrest or violence of any sort.'
>
> (Brittain and Minty 1988: 8)

Here is a child perfectly capable not only of rational thought but also able to offer a complex analysis of the horrors he experienced.

After the horrors of apartheid in South Africa the new government had an enormous number of issues to address and included in these was the protection of the rights of children. Built into the constitution which was ratified in 1996 was a bill of rights that guarantees children four rights – to survival, to development, to protection and to participation. And in the new curriculum developed for all schools it is set out that the purposes of language in the curriculum include the categories *political* and *critical*. Political gives all children the right to assert or challenge power, persuade others about the viewpoints of other people and to develop and sustain identities. Critical gives all children the skills to understand and challenge the relationship between language, power and identity and to understand the dynamic nature of culture and to resist persuasion.

The notion of an 'everybaby'

The type of scientific approach to studying child development is based exclusively on observations and experiments carried out in North America and Europe. It is important to note that only 18 per cent of the world's children live in these areas and the studies were carried out primarily on the children of white middle-class parents – which represents an even smaller percentage. Yet so pervasive have these findings been in schools and universities in the developed world that a notion of universality has emerged. It is as though Piaget's typical child is a model for all children, or what Gottlieb (2004) calls 'an everybaby'. There are sociologists, cultural psychologists and anthropologists who would question whether universality –which implies ignoring context and history – can properly be applied to a study of children.

You may well be familiar with the notion of developmental milestones. Much has been written about these and the suggestion that children reach particular milestones at particular ages is possibly another feature of 'everybaby'. It is interesting then to note that studies in Africa suggest that the ages at which African children reach particular behavioural milestones indicate that they develop at a faster rate than American children. Can this possibly be so? Richter and Griesel (1994) have shown that South African infants have significantly higher psychomotor and mental development scores on the Bayley Scales of Infant Development. Possible reasons put forward to explain such differences include looking closely at child-rearing practices, some of which include things like carrying the infant in an upright position, which may foster earlier neuromuscular development. The details are interesting but the suggestion that development will vary according not only to individual and group but also to culture and context is vital. Two case studies illustrate the wide differences between children of the same age, growing up in different contexts and cultures:

> Two-year-old Zakes is sent to the market to buy things and has routine jobs to do within the context of his African family. For example he sometimes takes messages to the neighbours and often helps with the cleaning and the cooking of food. Independence is fostered.

> Two-year-old Alex has no role to play within his family. He has his own room, equipped with many toys and is often to be found watching cartoons on the video. He sleeps in a child's bed, has low chairs to sit on and has no independence.

In later chapters we will explore in depth the impact and importance of culture and context.

The child as individual

Child development studies in the developed world are characterised by the notion of the ideal child as an individual. We are used to considering the importance of each child – thinking about each child's preferences, fears, experiences, strengths and weaknesses. Educators in the developed world promote ideas of self-confidence and self-esteem, separateness and individuality.

But this, too, is not universal. For many children the notion of the group and the community is essential to thriving and survival. Penn (2001) cites the examples of children in Mongolia who are taught to consider the needs of others and to avoid noise, disturbance and discord. Similarly LeVine (2003) speaks of communities where children are expected to develop self-restraint and mutual tolerance.

Closely associated with the concept of the ideal individual child are notions of consumerism because the individual child's tastes and needs must be catered for through the provision of specialist toys, foods and possessions. A walk around a nursery school in the developed world will reveal the wide range of materials, equipment and toys specially designed to meet the perceived needs of young children as they make sense of their world. In Southern India, Viruru (2001) describes a typical nursery where frugality is what underpins the pedagogical approach. This is not because there is insufficient money to purchase specialist play materials. Rather, the underpinning philosophy is that material possessions are unimportant and that a good Hindu should not be overwhelmed by worldly goods.

The implications

Piaget, with his strong emphasis on the active learner, presented an image of the generic child as male – a constructor, an explorer and an individual in control of his own learning and his environment. This was almost inevitable when one considers the time and place of his work. Nonetheless, critics including Cannella and Viruru (ibid.) suggest that the female learner – although still potentially acquiring logico-mathematical reasoning – may receive contradictory ideas from society and culture, things associated with independence, individuality, reasoning, negotiation, compromise, passivity and/or dependence. They also argue that the emphasis on individuality may allow for the denial of group issues like gender, but also of class, race and culture. Walkerdine (1988) was convinced that Piaget's logic, although designed to promote a rational and democratic society, also created a generic child 'to meet the egocentric, ethnocentric needs of the European male child' (Cannella and Viruru 2004: 94). Finally, there is the issue of Piaget's child-centredness which may create nothing more than an illusion of freedom. The question critics need to ask is whether this freedom applies not only to Piaget's ideal child but also to those who are not male, nor white, nor adult, nor always rational.

The importance of brain studies

There has been a considerable amount of publicity given to recent neuroscientific research. The development of non-invasive techniques like magnetic resonance imaging (MRI) for seeing what happens in the human brain has allowed an understanding of some issues – that certain nutrients are essential for foetal and neonatal growth, for example – and a gross oversimplification of others. Put simply, research has been interpreted to suggest that the human brain is most malleable in the early years of life when synaptic connections are laid down. These connections – described as the essence of learning itself – are said to be laid down as a consequence of stimulation, and stimulation itself has become regarded as the nutrient for learning. Educational programmes proliferate, suggesting that mothers and later caregivers and educators should stimulate their babies and children in order to enhance learning. In effect there is little real foundation for this. The evidence of neural connectivity is scant and the notions of stimulation are bound by culture and class. One of the most severe critics of the assumptions made about neuroscientific evidence is Rose (1998). He suggests that what we know is little and the technology is still in the early stages of development and too primitive to justify the claims made (and the money for intervention programmes that have followed). We will return to the whole area of brain studies later in this book.

Summing up

In this chapter we have looked primarily at the work of Jean Piaget and at his thoughts on how children come to make meaning through their explorations of the world. You may have noted that in his work with its emphasis on the individual child and on a linear path towards rational thought, there is little mention of the role of others in learning. Piaget saw the child as active constructor of knowledge and believed that this constructive process was universal and came about through the interaction between the individual learner and the physical environment. His is a complex theory and a very influential one, despite criticism of many aspects. He is possibly prime amongst the theorists known as constructivists. We have looked, too, at those who criticised his work and at how the notion of the little scientist, the universal child, does not allow us to account for the huge diversity we encounter when we broaden our palette to encompass all the world's children. In the next chapter we turn our attention to the work of theorists who might be described as social constructivists.

Questions

- How, if at all, have you had to re-evaluate your ideas about the contribution made by Piaget to an understanding how children learn and develop?
- What is your response to the notion of an 'everybaby' – a universal child?
- Do you see the human infant as a miniature scientist or do you notice and miss the absence of fantasy and pleasure in such models?

Chapter 3

The child as social constructor

In this chapter we move on to looking at the child as a member of the social world. There are two distinct aspects to this. The first is the role that others (both peers and adults) play in the learning and development of the child and the second is how the child comes to understand the social world. The key theorist whose work we look at in this chapter is the Russian psychologist, Lev Vygotsky.

> Fatih and Darinder are both in a nursery. They are three years old. They are playing with magnets. An adult is watching them. The children use the magnet to try and pick up some objects — a wooden toothpick, a plastic glue pot, a sponge. Nothing happens. Then Fatih tries a paper clip and a metal pencil sharpener and when the sharpener starts to move towards the magnet he is delighted. The adult asks 'I wonder why that is happening?' Darinder wants to have a go and then says to Fatih 'Some things worked, didn't they and some didn't.' They decide to sort the things on the table into two piles — those that stick and those that don't. After a while the children use the magnet to pick up all the metal things and they comment that some things are still on the table. The adult asks why and Darinder replies 'They haven't got the right things, the right bits to make them stick.'
>
> Marianna is crying in a corner of the playground, She is new to the school and doesn't yet speak any English. Four-year-old Bongiwe came to the school six months previously and also spoke no English. She notices Marianna's distress and goes over to one of the teaching assistants and says 'Marianna — she crying. She sad. No English'.

These examples illustrate the two strands of understanding the social world that we will explore in this chapter.

In the last chapter we examined, in depth, the views of one of the founding fathers of Western theories of child development, Jean Piaget. In our examination of some of his key themes we found some that supported our portrait of the twenty-first-century child. Piaget gives us a child who, from birth, is actively engaged in making sense of the world and is intent on experiencing it. She is able to make her own personal maps which can be considered as Piaget's repeated patterns of behaviour which become internalised and later allow her to remember her previous experiences. The picture we have is of a child very much situated at any time and in any place. Context and culture play little part and although Piaget gave some weight to both biological factors (what the child inherits) and to social/environmental factors (what the child experiences), the importance of others in the development of the child was rarely addressed.

It is evident that social context is very marginalised in much of the psychology written up to the 1970s when a more critical psychology began to emerge. This approach was wary of a psychology based on universal laws which were supposed to apply at all places and times. Radically, the Russian psychologist Lev Vygotsky, writing in the Soviet Union in the 1920s, adopted a much more social and cultural view of learning and development and this was consistent with his views on Marxist dialectical materialism. His deep concern was to explain development in terms of both biological and social concerns. Central to his approach was the notion of mediated action.

Mediated action: the role of others in learning

By *mediation* Vygotsky was talking about the use of communicable systems (by which he meant the ways in which ideas and thoughts could be communicated by one person to another or to groups of others) both for representing reality and for acting on it. He saw this as the basis of all cognition. This model goes way beyond the simple stimulus response model we discussed in the first chapter. For Vygotsky the role of others in learning was essential and by others he meant adults but also, crucially, other children. He believed that during socialisation (interacting with others) the child was inducted or drawn into the culture and then internalised the means of being part of that culture through the very fact of their common participation in activities with others. So sharing something with another person allowed the child to take the first steps in becoming a member of the shared culture of that interaction. These ideas are quite difficult to understand at first, but as you read on you will be able to see just what it is that Vygotsky was arguing.

It is society, he believed, that produces the *symbolic tools* or the communicative systems. These may be material or linguistic and are what shape the development of thinking. So the child is born into a culture and becomes a full member of that culture through making meaning of all aspects of that culture – the practices and beliefs and values. The child does this through using the communicable systems as tools which allow the child's thinking to change. Vygotsky said that

> The inclusion of a tool in the process of behaviour (a) introduces several new functions connected with the use of the given tool and with its control; (b) abolishes and makes unnecessary several natural processes whose work is accomplished by the tool; and (c) alters the course and individual features (the intensity, duration, sequence, etc.) of all the mental processes that enter into the composition of the instrumental act, replacing some functions with others (i.e. it re-creates and reorganises the whole structure of behaviour just as a technical tool re-creates the whole structure of labor operations).
>
> (Vygotsky 1981: 139–140)

Confused? The language itself is difficult to unpack, but please read on in order to make meaning for yourself. Vygotsky talked a lot about tools and by tools he meant things like the everyday tools we use such as pens and pencils but also things we might be surprised to find called tools – such as words and paintings and music. And because he was interested in how ideas and knowledge were passed on from generation to generation, he was interested in the particular tools that define a culture. For Vygotsky, then, artefacts or cultural tools transform mental functioning and affect thinking.

- The book the child hears read to her creates pictures in her head which change her thinking.
- The marks the child sees an adult make on paper raise questions and change thinking in the child's head about what it is the adult is doing.
- The ringing sound of the mobile phone makes the child consider whose voice might be at the other end.

The development of thinking (or of the mind) comes about through the interweaving of the biological (what the child has inherited) and the appropriation of the cultural or material heritage of the child which exists in the child's society. The artefacts or tools which allow the child entry into the culture have been created by the people in the child's society over time. So this is how children acquire and become part of culture – which includes beliefs, language, norms, artefacts, ways of acting and so on.

This is a difficult concept to grasp but one that makes perfect sense once grasped. A key symbolic tool is language. This is clearly a communicative system and it changes the relationships of human beings to one another. But there are other tools that we have developed and used and these all shape our thinking.

Here are some examples:

- various counting systems
- mnemonic devices for remembering
- algebraic symbols
- paintings and sculptures
- music
- maps and diagrams
- conventional signs.

Examples of people using such tools include:

- the Incas tying knots in strings to create a record of time;
- young children learning to chant nursery rhymes;
- the icons used to show emotional states on mobile phones and computers.

Vygotsky's theory was based on the premise that all knowledge and all the knowledge-making tools (about which we have been talking) available to a community reside within a sociohistorical context. Your community and mine each has a set of beliefs and practices which govern the way in which the world operates and that have been developed over generations and which collectively represent its history. My community includes being an immigrant, being a non-believer, valuing reading and music and education, enjoying Middle Eastern food, speaking English and some other languages, enjoying families and so on. Your community will probably share some but not all of these beliefs and ways of operating. The ways in which the beliefs and customs are passed down from generation to generation are through the language and the symbolism used to communicate these whilst they are being made part of the culture through participation. I sat alongside my grandfather whilst he chanted Yiddish rhymes. You may have worked alongside your mother making pasta or alongside your siblings going to Sunday School or watching your mother dress in her burkha.

According to Vygotsky all children born into communities can be viewed as gradually appropriating to themselves the knowledge and the psychological tools of the people who make up their community. This is a way of making the knowledge gained through interaction the child's own. So the child assumes ownership of this knowledge through internalising it. Vygotsky went on to theorise that this internalisation took place twice, on two planes, first on the *social* level, and then on the *psychological* level or personal, internal level.

Put more simply, what he was saying was that learning or cognition happened first through interaction and then by internalisation. Learning first takes place through being alongside more experienced others and second through internalising or making mental images or maps of what has been experienced and understood. In light of this we can say that *the acquisition of knowledge and the making of meaning may best be viewed as being socially and culturally determined rather than as individually constructed.* We are moving away from the lone rational scientist to the collaborative learner. This is an important idea and it is worth reading it again.

There now follows an example to illustrate what happened when two little girls started to talk about death and dying. In the setting of a Swedish preschool, three-year-old Maja and four-year-old Karin are engaged in a play sequence which lasts for about 15 minutes. They have built a hut of blankets and pillows. The play sequence starts with the children pretending to be friends at bedtime when they start to talk about being ill. They pretend to go to sleep and then Karin pretends to be a princess and Maja her mother. The extracts of dialogue that follow are quoted from a piece of research carried out by Annica Lofdahl at Karlstad University.

Karin: I was ill too, because I was soon going to die ...
Maja: Mmm
Karin: That's why I am in ... I am in the grave

...

Maja: You have to die first because you can be buried

(Lofdahl 2005: 11)

Maja then suggests to Karin that she could die if she jumped from the chute on which the hut was constructed. Karin does not agree at first but later changes her mind as the play continues. Later Karin realises that she must be dead before she can be buried and is eager to convince Maja that she really is dead. Now that they have reached consensus the play can continue into its final sequence – the funeral.

The whole piece is worth reading because it clearly illustrates how the children – peers, sharing their play culture – use language in order to explore unfamiliar ideas and how they create new and shared meanings for knowledge to be acquired. This is a clear example of one of Vygotsky's key themes, that of children learning from others – either peers or adults.

Barbara Rogoff (2003) takes the argument about mediation a stage further. She argues that development occurs on three rather than on the two planes described by Vygotsky. She did a lot of work in the US but also with communities in developing countries where she noted how children were more involved in the real life of families and community, and were involved in the processes, routines and rituals of the adults. She watched as children were inducted into the practices of families and communities through what she called *guided participation*. This guided participation was sometimes through being alongside an experienced person watching what they were doing, sometimes through social interaction such as talking about what was being done and sometimes through direct teaching. Her view of development now involves three interacting planes at which development occurs. These are the *individual plane* within the child him- or herself; the *social plane*, involving other people within the community within which he or she lives, and the actual *sociocultural context* which defines the manner in which these people engage in the processes of making and sharing meaning. So Rogoff extends to the personal and social planes the sociocultural plane.

> Three children are alongside their mother who is making tortillas on the fire. She gives them each a lump of dough and they watch what she is doing and imitate her, throwing the dough, flattening it and rolling it. They watch their mother but also one another. Here they are doing and memorising individually as they are involved with other people within the cultural context of making the bread of their community.

In Rogoff's words, development 'is a process of people's changing participation in the sociocultural activities of their communities' (Rogoff 2003: 52). This is important because it means that we cannot see development itself as a universal term. Rather, development must involve the acquisition of those skills and knowledge practices which are important to the host (in the sense of the particular) community rather than to a generalised community.

Piaget versus Vygotsky: is there a dichotomy?

In much of the literature there is an implied division between the thoughts of Piaget and those of Vygotsky on the importance of the social dimension to learning and development. Piaget's views are summarised as the individual child constructing knowledge through his or her own actions on the world. By contrast Vygotsky is said to believe that understanding is social in origin. As in many dichotomies this is an oversimplification of the views of both. In many places in his work Piaget explicitly recognised that the social world is a co-equal in the construction of knowledge. As early as 1932 he talked about societies being made up of relations and being not fixed but incomplete and in 1970 he said: 'there is no longer any need to choose between the primacy of the social or that of the intellect: collective intellect is the social equilibrium resulting from the interplay of the operations that enter into all cooperation' (Piaget 1970: 114).

Vygotsky was, of course, deeply interested in the importance of the social world but also saw the child as active constructor of knowledge. Some of this is evident when he discusses Piaget's notions of how children acquire language and, as part of this hugely complex process, use *egocentric speech*. By egocentric speech Piaget was talking about the personal narratives or running commentaries that young children often use. Vygotsky noticed that the child's use of egocentric speech whilst doing something practical itself affected the child's thinking. So the use of a communicative system (spoken language) was both a tool for learning and later a tool for thinking about what had been learned.

> Three-year-old Minna is playing with dough on the kitchen table. Her mother is in the same room talking to a friend. The adults are intrigued to note that Minna talks aloud all the time she is playing.

'I throw it on the table. Whoops. What a noise. I feel it – soft, squishy. Lovely and cold. I throw it again. Whoops! Loud noise ... Oh no!, some dirty bits here. I'll get a tissue to make it clean again ... Rub, rub. Look, the tissue bits are sticking to my dough. I'll put it in the fridge to get clean'.

The child is talking aloud through her actions, both describing them and analysing them in terms of the effect of what she is doing. At the end of this session (very abbreviated here) she notices that her attempt to clean the dough with the tissue has not worked and comes up with her own theory for what might work – putting the dough in the fridge.

The zone of proximal development

For Vygotsky, as we have said, learning was the social transmission of knowledge. He believed that all learners operate at two levels. The first is the *performance* level and is what the child demonstrates that he or she can do unaided. The second is the level of *potential development* and this can be achieved with the guidance and support of an adult or in collaboration with a more capable peer. Vygotsky described the gap between these two levels as the *zone of proximal development* (ZPD). For Vygotsky what was demonstrated at the performance level was what the child has already mastered. What is at the upper level demonstrates functions that are not yet mature but are in the process of becoming so. He famously stated: 'What the child can do with assistance today she will be able to do by herself tomorrow' (Vygotsky 1978: 87). It is obvious that this aspect of Vygotsky's work has implications for those involved in teaching. He was interested in the relationship between learning and development and felt that in order for the learning opportunities available to a child to be of use to development they must be appropriately targeted. This means that offering opportunities at or below the performance level will not bring about learning because the child's cognitive functioning here is stable and mature. Equally, it would be useless to offer opportunities above the top of the ZPD level because the difference from the child's actual level of functioning might be too great. So the art of effective teaching and what is sometimes called 'good learning' (Meadows 1993) is learning which is only slightly in advance of development. Wertsch and Stone (1985) state that teaching is good only when it 'awakens and rouses to life those functions which are in a stage of maturing, which lie in the zone of proximal development' (Wertsch and Stone 1985: 165).

The question for the educator – and this includes, of course, parents, carers and others involved in the development of the child – is what is it that the adult (or more proficient peer) should do to ensure learning. Another theorist, and this time a British one, Jerome Bruner, now enters the frame. In an attempt to understand and explain the ZPD he offered the concept of 'scaffolding' learning. His explanation was that it is the work of the adult or more proficient learner to act as the consciousness of the learner until such time as the learner is in control of his or her learning. Once the child has achieved this mastery he or she is able to function independently and the new function or conceptual system becomes 'his or hers' and the child can then use it as a tool. You can see how Bruner builds on much of what Vygotsky has told us. So the educator offers a scaffold of small steps alongside the child to help the child internalise external knowledge and then turn that into a tool to be used for conscious control.

Again, the language and concepts appear difficult, but in effect scaffolding is something that adults and proficient learners often do almost instinctively. Implicit in this model is a gradual move from other-regulation or control to self-regulation as the child moves towards the upper limit of the ZPD. As the child makes this journey the adult, at first, may have to give help and support which is explicit and frequent; later the help will be more abbreviated and less frequent. Here is an example of scaffolding:

> Yinka is trying to make a model out of coloured blocks, following a template which arrived in the same box as the blocks. His mum, alongside him, pays attention to what he is doing and gives him detailed and precise advice.' Look, now you need a blue one' and 'You need one exactly the same as that one' (pointing).
> Two days later he tries to do the same thing, this time moving more quickly through his construction. Towards the end – where he is required to balance one block on another – his mother offers less explicit advice.' Can you remember how you did it last time?' and 'What do you think you could do?'

In this example the child is gradually being helped to internalise what he has done (hence become conscious of what he can do) and then helped to find ways to know what to do next. He is moving from being largely dependent on the help of someone else to being less dependent on the less explicit and less detailed help and will soon need no help at all.

A sociocultural theory of psychological processes

Like Piaget, Vygotsky was a constructivist in that he perceived of the child as constructing meaning from experience. But over and above that he emphasised that children choose and use tools that are socially constructed. In the nursery schools of Reggio Emilia the children often choose to represent their understanding through painting or drawing. They select this cultural tool and it is significant that in some of the nurseries there is an artist in residence. Children can visit the artist in the atelier and watch what he or she is doing. There are also framed paintings displayed throughout the nurseries. In the reception classes in England young children are expected to represent their understanding through writing. This is the dominant cultural tool in the culture of the school. It is apparent that there is a cultural and historical pattern built into cognition. One of Vygotsky's colleagues, Luria, studied what was happening in the 1930s in agricultural regions in central Asia. He was looking for evidence that there were differences between the cognitive processes used by the literate in the cities and those used by the illiterate and uneducated peasants. His analysis of what he found was criticised for being pejorative about peasant society. He suggested that the ways in which peasants classified and sorted objects in their lives was inferior to the sorting into clear categories more evident in educated societies. Later consideration, however, suggested that functional sorting of artefacts was culturally significant (e.g. sorting out clothes so that they would not be eaten by moths, putting food into sealed jars to keep out insects, storing tools on a high shelf out of the reach of children) and not less cognitively significant for development. It is worth thinking about how many of the ways in which we sort and categorise objects are determined by the demands of education rather than of culture. Think about how many times you find children in nurseries and schools being asked to sort things by colour or shape or size for no particular reason.

It is here that ideas around the concept of 'activity' arise. Vygotsky believed in socially meaningful activity. As a Marxist he was concerned with activity which would offer some benefits to the group, the culture, the society. Early childhood educators often talk about meaningful activities and by this they mean activities which will make *human sense* to children. Human sense was a term used by Donaldson (1978) who believed that much of what young children are asked to do in schools is decontextualised and abstract and the purpose of the activity is not clear to the learner. Think about asking children to complete a worksheet which requires them to colour in all the triangles red and all the squares blue. The teacher's goal is apparent to us. She or he wants to check that the child can identify two different shapes and colours (and, perhaps, can colour in neatly). For the child this cannot be described as a meaningful activity. Contrast it with the child, at play, setting the table and spontaneously looking for another red saucer to match those she has put on the table. Here the purpose, defined by the child, makes human sense to her; there is a purpose to it.

Intersubjectivity

This chapter is entitled 'The child as social constructor' and so far we have looked at the child as constructor of the world with help from others — i.e. in social contexts. Our focus has been on how the child comes to understand the physical world. We now turn our attention to how the child begins to make sense of the social world. In other words we now begin to look at how the child develops concepts of him- or herself as distinct from others, but in relation to others. One of the key themes here is that of *intersubjectivity*.

It is apparent that the human infant is interested in and responsive to the emotions and the behaviour of others. Colwyn Trevarthen (1977) showed that infants as young as two months of age showed a different response to someone who spoke to them than to someone else in the room who was silent. Johnson (1990) showed that newborn infants pay closer attention to an object with a face-like arrangement of blobs on it (eyes and mouth) than to an identical object with abstract patterns on it. It seems that human development is almost naturally social, in the sense that humans are inclined to react socially in cultural contexts and to both make and share meaning. Those who adopt this view of development see relationships and communications with others as the most significant feature of the child's environment.

Trevarthen (1995) goes further and looks at how children come to learn the culture into which they have been born. He asks why it is that very young children are so keen to learn the language and all the other habits and customs and rituals and beliefs of the community around them. He says that a three-year-old child is a socially aware person who can make and keep friends, who can negotiate and co-operate with many different people in many different situations. For Trevarthen young children primarily make sense by sharing. They use their emotions and the emotions of others to categorise experiences that will help them co-operate. For many years Trevarthen has been analysing, in minute detail, videos of infants and their mothers and in doing this he has been made aware of some things that made him turn to a concept first introduced by the philosopher Habermas. The concept is that of intersubjectivity and a common-sense definition of intersubjectivity is having a shared understanding. This definition makes clear how important it is for both partners to come to a shared understanding of both the issue and the intention.

Trevarthen, like many theorists in the developed world, was interested in the early interactions and bonds between mother (or primary caregiver) and infant. Before the infant acquires language, interactions take place around objects or events and are very much to do with what is happening in the here and now between the mother (or caregiver) and the infant. Each is responding to the other and they are commenting on what is happening, in the sense of showing affect or emotion.

The mother tickles the baby: the baby chuckles: the mother smiles and tickles the baby again.

Trevarthen believed that what is happening in these dance-like exchanges is a growing awareness in the infant of the feelings or the emotions of the mother. He called this *primary intersubjectivity*.

This simple exploration of the feelings of others begins to develop at around nine months of age. It is then, Tomasello (1997) noted, that the mother follows the child's gaze to determine what the child is interested in or paying attention to (or vice versa with the child following the mother's gaze or actions). Attention becomes shared around what is being focused on and it is this shared focus of attention that now moves beyond the here-and-now interaction into the world of objects – perhaps toys, or food or other people.

Uri looks at his mother and sees her looking out of the window. He sees the car out of the window and points to it. 'Yes', says the mother, interpreting the question he cannot yet ask through following the child's gaze. 'Your daddy's home'.

Trevarthen called this *secondary intersubjectivity* and believed that its importance was that it allowed the infant to develop a realisation that the events and the things in the world, and the actions made on or with these, can be experienced by more than one person. Goncü (1998) states that the importance of this is that it prepares the child to share meanings with peers and it is through their new symbolic competence that children can construct and develop intersubjectivity in peer interactions. This involves them in discussion, negotiation, sharing meaning and collaborating. We saw a fine example of this in the example about the funeral stated earlier and you will encounter many more examples in the chapter on role play.

This brings us – for the first time – to considering the importance of play, particularly of social pretend play. What children do when they pretend is that they use physical, psychological or symbolic ways of representing the meaning of something. There is a well-known video sequence produced many years ago by the Open University which shows a little girl called Helen playing as the 'manager' of a canteen. This four-year-old clearly is not the manager of anything, but in her play she demonstrates that she has incorporated some of the language, the gestures, the intonation patterns, the ways of interacting that sum up for her someone with an important role to play. Where she has gained these ideas from is open to debate. Perhaps her mum is a manager; perhaps she has watched how the nursery teacher behaves; perhaps she watches her older sister being bossy. But she has clearly worked out some behaviours that define for her what it means to be in charge and she uses the words and actions to represent her understanding of the role. When two children join together in collaborative pretend play they have to agree on the reference and on the appropriate ways of being the people they have chosen to be. Goncü tells us that when trying to analyse what happens in pretend play we can turn, again, to Trevarthen. For the play to be successful the children have to have a shared focus of attention. They have to agree on certain things relating to what the play will be about and what parts need to be played. Are they both going to be fairies? Is one going to be the doctor and the other a patient? Who should be the mother and who the baby? They need to coordinate and share intentions and these are cognitively complex issues to resolve.

There is something else that happens at around nine months of age and that is the beginning of *self-awareness*. When the child is able to follow the gaze of the mother there is the suggestion that the child is realising that the mother can look independently just as the child can. This leads on to imitation and more complex behaviours and action. Between about fifteen months and two years most infants will recognise themselves in a mirror. Some theorists (e.g. Meltzoff and Gopnick 1993) suggest that this indicates the beginning of self-consciousness and this may be illustrated by the child hiding behind the mother because of feeling shy or awkward. This may be the first indication of the infant having a sense of him- or herself living in a social environment where others may have a view of them.

In this social world of ours children are constantly involved in acting and communicating in exchanges with others. This is where meaning is shared. Rogoff (1990) suggests that what happens in these exchanges is a blend of internal and external. Whatever is the focus of shared attention, let us take a book as an example, we cannot say that the book belongs to the mother or to the child. Where the mother reads to the child and points to the book, the meaning of a concept (perhaps there is a dog eating a bone, or a baby crying, or wild things swinging from trees) must be negotiated if there is to be shared understanding. Rogoff thinks that what happens is that the child appropriates or takes in something from the shared activity and is able to use this in later activities – alone or in participation. It is her belief that social exchanges themselves are the medium for social activities to be transformed and used by individuals according to their understanding and their involvement. Wertsch and Stone (1979) tell us that the process actually becomes the product. Communication and shared solving of problems may bridge the gap between what is already known and what is to be learned.

The impression may have been given that this learning will lead to a mere repetition of what is known, but Rogoff argues that the child here is actively constructing his or her meaning and is thus engaged in a *creative process*. Here we return to some of the ideas discussed in the previous chapter as we examine children's increasing ability to use analogy as a tool of thinking. There are many examples in the literature, of children engaged in discussion or dialogue, where they demonstrate a striking ability to make connections between ideas. Rogoff offers a startling example of two sisters, aged four and seven, with their mother. It starts over a pizza when the four-year-old asks her mother where they all came from and how they came to be alive. The discussion moves from 'from your mother and father who came from their mother and father' to the seven-year-old volunteering that long ago there were no people, only apes and that all people were descended from apes. The discussion then moved on to talking about where apes came from, and where dinosaurs came from, right down to one-celled creatures. When the mother then asked the girls where these one-celled creatures came from the older girl volunteered the response 'From ENERGY'. The mother was stunned to learn that this response arose from a conversation the girls had had with their grandfather two weeks before. Here is seven-year-old Luisa's explanation (note that doodle-doodles was the term used by Grandpa for electrons and neutrons and doodle-doodle-doodles the term for quarks and neutrinos):

> Well, Grandpa told me that molecules ... were made up of atoms, and atoms were made up of doodle-doodles ... and those were made up of doodle-doodle-doodles ... and *they* were made from ENERGY, just energy. So, I just figure that energy is what the one-celled animals came from
>
> (Rogoff 1990: 200)

Constructing the social world: what children need to know and do

In order to build a picture of a world made up of other people, children need to begin to construct representations to explain to themselves how others feel, what they want and need, what rules operate to hold their society together and what other people may be thinking. One of the most significant contributors to our understanding of this is Judy Dunn, whose seminal book *The Beginnings of Social Understanding* (1988) is still a key reference text. Dunn spent time observing young children (a recognised and valued way of studying children and their development). Much of her work involved looking at young children in the settings of their home. She found some very interesting things, many of which are in direct contrast to Piaget's views. Piaget, as you will remember, believed that young children were unable to decentre or take on the point of view of others.

Dunn tells us that children are not just passive partners in interactions with others, but are active participants. This means that when they engage in relationships and interactions with parents, family members, other children and other people like teachers or doctors or neighbours, they work hard at making sense of the feelings, the needs, the intentions and the goals of these others. This is to allow them to be able to function as members of their social group. So our mythical twenty-first-century child, as a player in her society, needs to explore the various systems with which she is involved – the nursery or setting, the home, the neighbourhood, the local clinic and so on. From early on she is actively making sense of the rules that make these systems viable.

In her book Dunn carefully illustrates how this takes place. We know that, from birth, the human infant is predisposed to learn about the characteristics of people, as we have seen through their attention to human faces and voices over other stimuli. At the age of only two months the baby can already differentiate between someone who wants to communicate with him or her from someone who is talking to another person. By the age of seven or eight months babies seem really attuned to different emotional expressions in adults and they begin to play co-operative games like peekaboo. This is a game with built-in routines and patterns and we examine the functions of these with regard to intersubjectivity later in this book. At this age babies share in the daily routines of feeding, changing, dressing and soon begin to demonstrate that they share a communicative framework with others – for example by waving goodbye, eye-pointing to what they want, or smiling with pleasure. They are highly social and sociable beings, intent on communicating with others. From the age of roughly eighteen months, children are able to understand how to hurt and comfort others; they understand the consequences of their own actions on others and something of what is allowed or not in the world of their family. They are also able to anticipate the responses of adults to their own misdeeds or those of others.

Dunn found that children's *understanding of the feelings* of others develops early in their second year of life. They start to respond empathetically to the distress of others and, she states, they are interested in the way others feel, exploring the causes of pain or distress, anger or pleasure, comfort or fear in themselves but also in others. They joke and play with and tell stories about these feelings and, she believes, the foundations for kindness are well established by the age of three.

> Eighteen-month-old Sarah hands her bottle of milk to the baby beside her on the bus who is crying inconsolably.

> Ben, aged two, seeing that his mother is distressed, asks 'Mummy crying?' To which his older sister replies 'No, mummies only cry when their daddies die'.

In terms of *understanding the goals of others,* Dunn illustrates how a sensitivity to the goals of others emerges in the play of two- and three-year-olds and enters into the stories they tell, the pretend games they play and the questions they ask.

> Three-year-old Emily is shocked when her mother screams and jumps on a chair when a mouse runs across the kitchen floor. 'Mummy, did you jump on the chair 'cos of the mouse? Are you scared, mummy?'

> Playing shops at home, three-year-old Rashida picks up a block and hands it to Ade to pay for the goods she is buying.
> Ade: Is this your money?
> Rashida: It's my credit card.
> Ade: Oh, plastic money. You must be buying lots of things.

From this comes an exploration of what makes some types of behaviour acceptable and others not. This implies that a set of social rules (specific to particular families and groups and societies and cultures) apply and children work hard in the early years to *understand these social rules.* Dunn's observations showed that between the ages of two-and-a-half and three children demonstrated some understanding of responsibility, and of excuses and explanations for why they have done things. Embedded in her observations is the evidence that children do notice and attend to the distress of others – a clear indication that young children can, indeed, decentre.

> Two three-year-olds are playing together in the bedroom of one of them. The visiting child, Leon, picks up a crayon and starts to draw on the walls. Mustafa shrieks in dismay 'No, no! You are not allowed to do that in my house. My mummy doesn't let me draw on the walls. We use paper.'

Finally, Dunn talks about how, in the course of their third year, children begin to talk about things like knowing and remembering and forgetting. They are talking about their own cognition and show an awareness that they are aware of their own minds and of *the minds of others.* She suggests that as children's thinking about the minds of others develop, this becomes more important to them than the simpler examinations of the feelings and goals of others.

Jacob (aged three): When we came to visit you in London you lived in a big house and we slept upstairs and you slept downstairs. And your car was red. And my daddy watched the television because he was missing Sydney and we played with those blocks you've got.

A nine-year-old child watched the interactions between a boy of about seven and the man sitting beside him on the train. 'I don't think he was his father because he asked him questions to things he would have known if he was his father. And I think the little boy was really sad. I wondered if something had happened to his mother'.

Development viewed in the contexts of place, time and culture

We have focused throughout this book on how development must always be viewed in the context of history, society and culture. Important too are things like climate and geography. In these examples we examine how children begin to construct the social world which is particular to them. Many of the world's children grow up in societies which adopt a collectivist approach where the focus is not on the individual, but on the individual in relation to others. A case study in point is that of the Nso children who live in the Bamenda Grassfields of Northwest Cameroon. Nsamenang and Lamb (1994) studied the socialisation of these children through interviews with volunteer parents and grandparents, carried out in the language of the Nso people, Lamnso. They found that Nso children, together with their families, are active participants in their own socialisation. The principles and values of their families include obedience and social responsibility, not individuality and the ability to express ideas verbally. They are still deeply rooted in their ancestral traditions, despite the impact of Westernisation on them. Much of the learning of the children comes about through guided participations, as described by Rogoff. You will remember that this is where children learn alongside adults or more experienced others, almost like apprentices. Nso children do play and they make their own playthings, and the process of making these things is thought to help them develop an image of themselves as creators or producers. Segall *et al.* note that 'The process of making these toys teaches the children how to plan work, organise tools and materials, to make measurements and to conceive of objects in three-dimensional space' (1990: 123). The example of cultural traditions like weaving, sculpture, embroidery, leather working and pottery is evident in what the children produce. You can see how the children use their cultural tools in order to make toys.

Nso children live in communities where the peer culture is powerful and this allows for peer mentoring and perspective taking, allowing children to develop their sensitivity to the needs and feelings of others, particularly of younger children. So the children play together and in this play they need to agree what their agenda is, to allocate and accept roles, and to understand the feelings of others and anticipate the impact of their actions or words on others. Older children have authority over their younger siblings and they are allowed to correct and reprimand them. So parents do not have sole responsibility for the affective and cognitive development of the children; children themselves are co-contributors to the socialisation of other children. It is suggested that Nso children learn to speak more from other children than from their parents. Stories and proverbs (other cultural tools) play an important role in educating the children into understanding the morality of the community – what is seen as right and wrong, for example. This is true of many cultures, as illustrated by the many stories with morals in them to be found throughout the world.

The families of the Nso children are extended families, as we have seen. Whatever families look like – and they vary enormously in their composition and structure – as you will know, there can be little doubt that they contribute enormously to child development. Barbarin and Richter (2001) examined what children need most from families in order to thrive and develop. They were looking at children in South Africa and the questions they asked included:

- Do families provide essential socialisation in terms of the values children need?
- Does the wealth of the family contribute significantly to the ability of the family to keep children safe and have their primary physical needs met?
- Is it the links and relationships and support within and between families that allow children to have a sense of belonging?

In this detailed study four separate analyses were carried out and the researchers themselves add a note of caution about over-interpreting the results. Nonetheless some of the findings give food for thought. In terms of children's social competence their findings suggest that where, within families, there were prosocial ways of resolving disputes, children's social competence developed. This means that in families where difficulties were dealt with positively and calmly, without anger or aggression, children were more likely to become socially competent. They also found that in smaller families, with fewer dependent children, children became more independent and socially competent.

Summing up

In this chapter we have looked both at how children learn more about their world through their interactions with others and at how they make sense of these others who inhabit their world. The key theorists mentioned in this chapter are Vygotsky, Bruner and Rogoff. So now our portrait of the twenty-first-century child has an added social and cultural dimension. She is learning through her interactions with family members, peers and others she encounters and she is also beginning to think about what it is that makes her distinct from but part of others. Through her interactions with others she is able to know that other people have needs and desires, likes and dislikes, minds and thoughts. She knows that within her culture some things are accepted and others not. She can empathise with others and share meaning with them.

Questions

- What do you now understand about how others – both adults and peers – mediate cultures and thus enable children to gain ownership of knowledge?
- What are your views on the roles of intersubjectivity in enabling young children to begin to share meanings, develop awareness of self and others and the feelings and goals of others. In your opinion is this making sense of the social world a creative process?

Chapter 4

The child as creative thinker

In this chapter we start to look at how the child, having constructed some views of the physical and the social worlds, starts to represent and re-represent these in order to be able to remember them, build on them and transform them to become progressively more complex understandings. In doing this we look at play, which is something children seem impelled to do, and analyse its importance in learning and development.

When Ola was ten weeks old she spent hours watching the mobile over her cot. She watched the movements with intense concentration. Some months later she started to enjoy some simple games that she played with her big sister who would hide her toys and say 'all gone!' and then make them pop up again. Ola always shrieked with delight.

When Ade was 13 months old he started to push any button he saw in the house to see what happened. If he liked what happened he pressed the button again. And again and again! His parents bought a new DVD player and he immediately went up to it and pushed the button and was delighted when lights came on.

Poppy, at 18 months old, has become a problem solver and an imitator. When the carer is cleaning she follows her around with her own cloth and is desperate to have a go with the broom and the dustpan. Her carer reported that when she wanted something out of reach she dragged her chair across the floor and then attempted to climb up on it.

Ahmed has few toys yet spends hours sorting out the things he finds. He makes collections of things that are, in some way, the same for him. His mother noted that yesterday he put lots of dark coloured objects together and light coloured objects in a different place. Today she saw him putting lots of stones in one place, sticks in another and dry leaves in a third.

Malika seems to be exploring the way in which some things will dissolve and others won't. She spends time putting water into some sand and stirring it. Then she tries putting water into gravel and stirring that to see what happens.

Tahiba is now starting to pretend. She takes an empty tin and pretends to have a drink out of it. Or she makes dolls out of scraps of fabric and carries them round, singing to them.

Making meaning of children's play

All these children are deeply engrossed in what they are doing. They are not engaged in trivial events, nor are they unable to concentrate over long periods of time. They are very busily engaged in trying to understand things about their world and as they do what they are doing they are asking questions in their minds and then seeking to find answers. This, for some of the children, is before they have spoken language so for them the whole process is about exploration of the objects they encounter through their senses and through physical exploration.

> Ola uses her eyes to track the movements of the mobile. What questions might she be asking? Why is it moving? What makes it move? Can I make it move? Will it stop moving?

As Ola does these things it is apparent that some questions are being raised in her mind and it is these that impel her to keep on exploring. Only she knows what she is seeking to discover.

> Ade is operating like a small scientist. He does something – makes some movement – and what he does creates some effect. If he likes what happened he tries again. He is discovering things about cause and effect.
>
> Poppy is acting as an imitator and as a problem solver. She watches what her carer does and then tries out that role for herself. Perhaps she wants to know what it feels like to be big and to be able to use a cloth to remove dust. Perhaps she wants to feel the soft cloth under her hands.

Any observation of children engaged in following their own interests will reveal the extremely serious and persistent nature of what they are doing and raise the question of what it is they are trying to make meaning of. What they are doing is not trivial nor is it necessarily 'fun'. They are clearly impelled in some way to explore what they encounter and to use whatever means possible to do so. These children are playing.

Defining play

Definitions of play abound. It was a concept talked about by Piaget and by Vygotsky and by many other theorists, all of whom conceded that it was an extremely significant feature of childhood and a way of learning. For Piaget play – like learning – was regarded as being developmental and moving from what he called *practice play*, through *symbolic play* and into *play of games with rules*. He believed that what children do is to use play as the way of unifying what they have experienced and learned (and they do this through assimilation), rather than adjusting to what they do not yet know through equilibration. This equilibration is always changing and this explains why play is a process and not a steady state. He was particularly interested in how play allowed children to explore rules and norms.

Vygotsky's zone of proximal development (first discussed in Chapter 3) is where the child can be assisted to move from his or her performance level to his or her potential level. Vygotsky believed that the zone of proximal development was created through play and here, children operate at their highest possible cognitive level. Vygotsky talked about children engaged in play standing a 'head taller' than themselves. By this he meant that in play, particularly in pretend play, children reveal more about what they know and can do than in other activities. Like Piaget he was interested in play as developing into games with rules, but with his emphasis on the social nature of development and learning, he focused on how every play sequence includes rules that the children must agree through negotiation. He noted that every game with rules contains imaginary aspects.

Bruner shared with Vygotsky an interest in play and he saw it as a way (or a mode) of learning and described it as an approach to doing something and not an activity in its own right. This echoes the idea that play is a process. This is an important and interesting point. What it means for us is that we should not see play as an activity in its own right but should realise that children can learn about aspects of language or mathematics or the physical world or the scientific world or anything else through play. Bruner, interested in the fact that the young of almost all mammalian species engage in play, regarded it as being 'non-serious' in the sense that the long period of human childhood relative to that of other species was precisely to allow the young human time for safe and playful exploration. He went on to suggest that without such playful exploration the development and use of tools would not have taken place. You will realise here that when he talks of tools he is doing so in the same way that Vygotsky did – talking about cultural tools like pencils and paintbrushes and scissors and books and computers as well as more traditional tools. This evolutionary approach to play is interesting, but not universally accepted. Bruner also believed that the 'in pretend' nature of play allows children to create alternatives to reality and in doing this they create symbols. In essence, in pretend play, the child simulates an action in play *as if* it were real, or the child tries out new combinations and sequences in a *what if* fashion.

> Martha is setting the table for a tea party in the home corner of her day nursery. She is behaving 'as if' she is having a real tea party and drawing on her previous experiences of seeing people set the table, or perhaps of going to a tea party or seeing what one might look like in a book or on a video or film.
>
> Hamish is climbing to the top of the climbing frame in the playground and looking out to see if he can spot the pirates whom he believes are just beyond the sandpit. He is behaving as though he is a sailor and acting out what he thinks a sailor would do.

Bretherton (1984) believed that pretend play was significant to learning and development. She stated that mental trial and error (thinking of different ways of doing things) and the ability to imagine (to engage in make-believe) were two facets of the same ability to represent the world. In other words, children need both in order to do things and to think about things symbolically. In the first example above Martha is setting the table and imagining a tea party. In doing this she is using metaphor in the sense that she is acting like someone who has a tea party. Hamish is climbing to the top and looking out and imagining a group of pirates. He, too, is using metaphor as he plays 'like a pirate'. Play, said Bruner, is *memory in action*.

Tina Bruce (1991) has written widely and influentially on play in early childhood education. In most of her work she talks not simply about play, but about what she calls *free-flow play*, which can be defined as spontaneous play. Bruce (ibid.) discusses two contrasting views of play. The first is what she calls the 'play as a preparation for life' approach and the second is 'play as an integrating mechanism'. In the first approach, play as a preparation for life, Bruce argues that the play is very much suggested and controlled by the adult. This can be illustrated by comments like 'Go and play in the home corner, Georgia' or 'Why don't you play with your game boy now?' In this approach, play may be described by the words 'fun' and 'happy'. Children are released from the drudgery of work in order to enjoy the perceived triviality of play. This question of play being pleasurable is a vexed one and we will return to it later.

Moyles (1998) has written much about play and does not limit her discussions to young children. She writers powerfully about the importance of the child having *ownership* of the play. What she means is that children choose what to do and thus control the agenda. They can become deeply engrossed in what they are doing and are able to change the agenda should things not go according to their original plan. In this way they cannot experience failure. She cites the work of Hutt *et al.* (1989), whose model focused on what children seemed to be doing as they played. Their work helps us to recognise that children's play is extremely complex. Despite the fact that play is such an important concept in Western views of children, in English we have only one word to cover a range of meanings. We use this word to describe things as diverse as playing a part, playing the piano, playing football, playing the fool, or playing at being something. Hutt *et al.* drew a distinction between *epistemic play* (play based around knowledge acquisition and involving an adult or more expert learner) and *ludic play* which we are calling pretend play or symbolic play or imaginative play. In their thesis, children in the earliest stages seem to ask 'What is this thing?' and then move on to asking 'What does this thing do?' and finally asking 'What can I do with this thing?' so moving from exploring objects and their properties through to exploring the functions of objects and then using objects to meet their own purposes. Where the player has ownership, the implication is that whatever it is that the player is doing is important to him or her. Here is an example:

> Rasheeda (3:9) wanders into the home corner, picks up a pencil which is lying next to a notepad beside the telephone. She picks up the phone and begins to talk as though she is taking a message. 'Just wait. I'll write it down'. She 'writes' some parallel squiggles on the notepad and says 'Now I won't forget. Bye, bye'. She then pretends to speak on the phone again, this time ordering a pizza. 'Hello. We want three pizzas – one for me and one for my brother and a big one for my mum'. She pauses and writes some lines on the pad, but this time adds the numerals 1 and 7. 'Our house is number 171.'

Rasheeda has chosen what to do so this is clearly an example of play. She has chosen to use the materials provided by the teacher in order to follow up her own interest in what 'taking a message' means. In the simplest terms we can say that she is exploring the uses of the telephone and how one records things on paper. She then moves on in her play to ordering a pizza and in her writing she includes two numerals – the numbers one and 7. On the next day Rasheeda was again observed:

> Rasheeda is playing with her friend Aaron in the writing area and they are getting very noisy. The teacher becomes irritated and asks (or rather tells) her to play with a jigsaw puzzle. Rasheeda grumbles about this, but being as helpful and malleable as many young children are, she complies and quickly completes a very simple puzzle. 'Done, miss' she announces and returns to giggling with Aaron.

This is an example of the child doing what she was effectively told to do by a teacher and despite the fact that she was told to 'play' with the jigsaw puzzle, this was not something that was either interesting or relevant to her. The consequence was that she was not engaged in the task and her behaviour cannot accurately be called play.

Our definition of play needs now to include the points listed below:

- Play is something the child has chosen to do. The child initiates the activity and in doing this is in control of his or her own agenda. The adult may play a role in the play. In the example of Rasheeda the adult selected the resources and these clearly influenced what Rasheeda chose to do.
- Play is often pleasurable and we often see children enjoying their chosen activity. In the example of Rasheeda she is clearly enjoying acting like an adult, taking messages and writing them down as she may have seen adults do. She is highly motivated to keep playing. But play can be frustrating and complex, so play may not always be pleasurable. It is likely to always be deeply engrossing. The child may spend long periods of time following up his or her concerns. In examples of children experiencing war, homelessness, cruelty and trauma they may still play but often their play is a way of acting out symbolically the terrible things they have experienced. In cases like this play is certainly neither fun nor pleasurable.
- In play there is no risk of failure. Since the child has chosen what to do and how to do it, if something goes wrong he or she can just change the agenda and do something else or do something differently.
- The emphasis is on the process rather than on the product. No one has asked Rasheeda to do or produce anything in the first example. The fact that she makes marks on paper is her choice.

Play as an integrating mechanism

You will remember that Tina Bruce describes play as an integrating mechanism and what she meant by this was that, in play, children draw on all their experiences and understanding, in order to both consolidate and create learning. She talked about children using their understanding of *rule formats* and of *scripts* and in doing this she referred to ideas of Bruner (1982) and Nelson (2000). Both of these writers had a strong focus on interaction and they considered the rule-bound nature of interactions between adults and children as useful sources for the child to draw on. So the child, in play, draws on all the available scripts or formats in order to explore a concern. We will discuss this in more detail in one of the following chapters.

We can go back to Rasheeda and try to identify the scripts she is integrating.

- Rasheeda has almost certainly seen and heard people on the telephone so she has a 'script' in her head for how this is done. She uses conventional English greetings like 'Hello' and 'Bye bye'.
- She has also heard people using the telephone for different purposes and has worked out that there are different formats or patterns for how this is done. You use a different tone and intonation for speaking to your mother than for speaking to the unknown person who is taking your order. The way in which she indicates she is taking a message is very different from the way in which she orders a pizza.

What we see is a child revealing her competence in 'acting like an adult' and in doing this she is integrating many of her previous observations, analyses, hypotheses and experiences.

Let us go back to the example of little Colin who, you may remember, used a ball to be a baby and the mop bucket to be the baby's pram. This is part of a long description of what took place.

> Anabel, aged four and a half, came over to Colin.
> 'Can I have the ball, Colin?'
> Colin looked at her. He seemed puzzled. She picked the ball up and kicked it away from her.
> 'Nooo!' Colin cried and ran after the ball ...
> Colin picked up the ball. 'Don't run away, baby. It's all right' he said lovingly. He then put the ball under his arm and pulled the bucket over to a small chair. He sat down on the chair and put the ball in the bucket. 'Going shops in a minute, baby, shops and sweets, baby, yeah?' he said.
> Later Colin went over to pick leaves from a bush in the corner and threw them into the pram for the 'baby', calling out 'Dinner baby.'
> Then when he had to go indoors to get his own dinner he was told to leave the ball outdoors. He wheeled the bucket with the ball in it into the shade, patted the ball and went in for lunch.
>
> (Allery 1998: 30)

The scripts and formats here are very different from those used by Rasheeda, but you will notice that Colin talks to the baby in the ways in which he has heard adults (and very possibly mothers) speak to babies. He has also noticed something about how to care for and show love for a baby. This is demonstrated by his putting the 'pram' in the shade and explaining to the baby what is happening, reassuring the baby that he or she is not being abandoned.

A significant factor about play that we have not yet mentioned is that it is very often in what we might call 'pretend' mode. Children know that what they are doing is not 'the real thing'. Rasheeda knows that no pizzas will arrive and that the message she has written down cannot be read by anyone. Colin knows the baby is a ball, the pram is a bucket and that he is not the baby's parent. The pretend nature of the play allows it to be pressure-free. This lack of pressure is extremely significant.

Imaginative/symbolic play

We would suggest that the young constructor of meaning uses play as a tool, just as he or she uses physical exploration, stories, observation of expert others, interaction and other means to make sense. Bruner believed that the thing that makes humans so distinctive as a species is that they create and use culture. *Symbols* are what make up culture. They can be defined as the building blocks of culture. It is apparent that different cultures use different symbols and that these symbols define aspects of that culture. The music, the food, the art, the artefacts and the beliefs are some of the symbols that define Turkish culture and they will be different from those defining Nigerian culture, for example.

In pretend play the child turns something into something else and thus in some way transforms reality. Bruner believed that pretend play or imaginative play must thus be seen as a form of representation. The child simulates an action in play as if it were real. Think of the child using a block as a telephone and speaking into it as if it were real or Colin treating his ball-baby so lovingly. Here we are considering children playing 'as if'. If we turn our attention to children playing 'what if' we see them trying out new patterns of action, and combining elements in order to create something new. Go back to Hamish on the look out for pirates and notice how he combines sequences of action with his image of what pirates might be like, where they might be hiding and what he, as an explorer or an adventurer, might need to do about it.

We have touched on how, after the earlier play with objects through sensorimotor manipulation, children begin to represent experience and become generative, as they play out activities they have experienced or seen others experience. Observing children engaged in symbolic play you will see them using simple pretence about themselves (using the block for a telephone); simple pretence about others (putting the doll to sleep); and then sequences of pretence (setting the table, cooking a meal, serving the meal). Some believe that pretend play moves from playing out *domestic* roles and sequences (mum, dad, baby, sister, brother, grandpa) to playing out *functional* roles (the teacher, doctor, nurse, train driver) to playing out *fantasy* or imaginary roles (fairy, Bionicles, dinosaur, witch). It seems too that children will sometimes engage in *solitary play* (and this is almost always the case with the youngest children) and may then move on to playing alongside others but not interacting with them (called *parallel play*) to playing with others (called collaborative or *co-operative play*).

Here are some examples:

> Three-year-old Simnikiwe has made a doll out of scraps of fabric. She wraps the doll in some large banana leaves and carries her round, singing to her. She is clearly playing the domestic role of mother. She is playing alone.

> A group of Guatemalan children of different ages are playing at cooking and serving a meal, using leaves to make tortillas and mud for the meat. They are playing domestic roles but moving towards functional roles of cooks and servers of food. They are playing together, sometimes collaboratively.

> Four children in a playgroup in East London are acting out a scenario where there has been a traffic accident. The play involves making the noises of ambulances. Two children become doctors and treat the other two who are told to lie on the ground and 'act dead'. This is collaborative role play where the script is agreed through negotiation. The roles played again include domestic and functional.

> Four little girls in the hills above a small Italian town are collecting seeds in order to make 'medicines' so that they can make the dolls better. The dolls have been laid out on the path. Functional roles are explored through social play.

> Jio has a long length of fabric and he is using it first to be a river he has to cross, then a magic cloak to keep him safe and then a bandage for his foot which he pretends has been bitten by a tiger. This child's solitary play does not depend on toys, but allows him to draw on his knowledge of traditional and new stories in order to explore things that interest

him – how to be strong in the face of terrible danger. This is total fantasy play where the roles he plays are neither domestic nor functional, but imagined.

Claims have been made about the links between children's competence in imaginary play and their cognitive abilities (e.g. Hughes 1995). In Western thinking, play has been elevated to a high status amongst early childhood experts and is regarded as the primary mode of learning in the Foundation Stage curriculum in the UK, for example. It is important to note that this is not the case in all cultures. In her book *Starting School: Young Children Learning Cultures* (2002) Liz Brooker looked at the views of play as a mode of learning held by two different groups of parents: white working-class parents and Bangladeshi parents. She focused on a reception class in a primary school which was described as having a child-centred approach to learning, emphasising the importance of children being able to learn largely through play. Hers was a small sample and the research was limited, but her findings are interesting and raise some important questions. She found that the English parents had taken on at least some of the rhetoric about children learning best through play, which they saw as quite distinct from teaching. Their children had many toys and were encouraged to play with them and to get dirty and to talk a lot. The Bangladeshi children had fewer toys and their parents saw play as something children did after they had learned. It seems essential then to include in discussion of play and learning a range of cultural dimensions.

Recently, in the developed world, there has been much talk of what is known as developmentally appropriate practice (DAP) which claims to draw on research and is often presented as the manual of current knowledge about young children. The research it draws on is almost entirely from the US and DAP makes no attempt to examine values or cultural perceptions in relation to children. It takes an age and stage stance, very much influenced by Piaget, and is prescriptive, telling parents as well as educators what to do. The second edition, produced in 1997, did take some account of difference and recognised the terrible effects of poverty, but the approach taken was still essentially consumerist in nature.

DAP promotes self-initiated and self-directed play, which are described as being the most effective ways of learning and are upheld by a rich resource base of materials, activities and the support of trained educators. This all presumes that there are universal and predictable sequences of growth and play. It totally ignores different patterns of child-rearing, different cultural expectations and practices, different lifestyles and most significantly different economic bases. There are several serious issues that arise from this.

The first issue is that through advocating a play-based approach to learning and development, play itself is misrepresented as being dependent on the level and quantity of resourcing which is not possible for the majority of the world's children. Viruru (2001)'s description of nurseries in Southern India was mentioned earlier and you will remember that there the decision not to offer a wide range of toys was a philosophical and not an economic one. The second issue is that parents can be taught to be 'good parents', implying the adoption of a model of parenting which is universalist. We arrive at the adult equivalent of 'everybaby' with 'everyparent'. Many in the developing world struggle to deal with the imposition this makes as educators, knowing little or nothing about particular cultures, particular routines and rituals, particular ways of child-rearing and interacting, seek to teach parents what to do.

Imaginative play in diverse cultural settings

It seems evident that children's play, like every aspect of their development, will vary according to their culture. Play is common in virtually all cultures but the way in which children play and the themes they adopt may be culture-specific. Roopnarine *et al.* (1994) found there were few detailed studies of imaginative play across cultures but since then studies are showing some interesting but not entirely surprising findings. Some studies have also looked at how mothers play and found that the ways in which they play and view play vary enormously. Rogoff *et al.* (1993) report that Guatemalan mothers will laugh with embarrassment if asked to play with their children as they see this as the role of other children or sometimes of grandparents. In Italy, mothers see play as inevitable but not requiring any adult intervention. In Turkey, as in the United States, Goncü and Mosier (1991) report that middle-class parents think of themselves as play-partners for their children. And this is the model being promoted by many of those involved with DAP, as we have seen.

In a recent study, Bernstein *et al.* (1999) looked at the exploratory and symbolic play of children under the age of two with their mothers from two cultures: Argentina and North America. They found that there were both similarities and differences in the play patterns they observed. In both groups boys engaged in more exploratory play than girls and girls in more symbolic play than boys. This was mirrored in the play of their mothers. In both there were individual variations in children's play and in each case this was closely related to the play patterns of the mothers. American children and their mothers engaged in more exploratory play than their Argentinean peers, but Argentinean mothers engaged more in social play with their children and gave more verbal praise to them.

One of the most frequently cited studies of cultural difference in symbolic play is that of Smilansky (1968). She looked at the play of two groups of Israeli children aged three to six. One group was described as of European descent and as middle class; the second as of North African descent and as lower working class. Smilansky found significantly less dramatic play in the group of lower-class children. By dramatic play she was talking about imitative play, pretend play with objects, social interaction and verbal communication. She suggested that this was due to the fact that the parents of these children knew less about play (you will notice value-judgements about parents, again!), valued it less, and had child-rearing techniques that did not promote the verbal and cognitive skills needed to develop imaginative play. No recognition was given to the pressures of the reality of the lives of the poorer families, of the impact of poverty, the importance of different norms and so on. Negative findings like these have since been challenged.

Roopnarine *et al.* (2000) remind us that recent studies move away from such a deficit view to a more analytical one, and find that children use pretend play in diverse contexts. In studies of observed play across India, Taiwan, Sierra Leone, Senegal and Guyana the following facts emerged:

- Children across these cultures (and certainly many others) can and do engage in elaborate role play during which they demonstrate that they sequence actions and adopt roles. Based on findings like this, Ebbeck (1972) suggests that accounts of imaginative play need to avoid making global assumptions and statements.
- Rates of symbolic play vary from culture to culture. Presumably this will be dependent on many factors, not least the economic position of the children and their

families and communities. Children contributing to the economic life of their family will have less time for symbolic play than those from more privileged homes.
• Play themes are more likely to involve roles and scripts related to family practices
and the everyday activities of cooking, working, cleaning, marketing, preparing
feasts, weddings, etc. rather than fantasy, although there is evidence of some fantasy
play.

What do children play about?

We have seen that pretend play is a representational activity and that when children
play in this mode they may use physical means (such as objects) or psychological
means (such as intonation patterns, and gesture) to represent the meaning of something else. We have seen how Helen, in the video clip mentioned earlier, playing at
being a manager, acted and spoke as she imagined a manager would. Once pretend
play becomes social (by which we mean it involves more than one child) it is essential
that children agree on the reference of pretence: they have to agree what it is they are
playing about and what they are doing in their adopted or assigned roles. We have
seen how this sharing of focus comes about through intersubjectivity. Here is an
example to illustrate this:

> Three four-year-olds are playing outdoors on the climbing frame. One shouts 'Be careful!
> There are crocodiles in the river'. The others look down (they are on the top bar of the
> climbing frame) and immediately 'see' the crocodile. This becomes the signal for how the
> play will progress.

Here the children clearly have a shared frame of reference. When one 'sees' crocodiles
the others know where to look and they also 'see' the crocodile. It is this imagined crocodile that becomes the focus of the play for the children. This is an extremely complex
cognitive act of shared meaning making.

The play scripts and scenarios children follow are often culturally or emotionally
determined. Many children use play as the vehicle for acting out – in safety- their deep-
est fears and concerns. Sometimes this is solo play and sometimes in collaboration.
Sometimes the root of the play is evident; often it is not.

> Three-year-old Maria was playing with the miniature figures in the doll's house in her
> nursery. Her family was going through a grave crisis and she acted some of the violence
> she observed and experienced at home by making the figures play the parts of family
> members.

> Two siblings, aged eight and ten, use their different toys and interests in combination to
> explore some common themes around friendships, loyalty, bullying and isolation. So Lego
> figures and dolls come together to act out play scripts: they go to school and act out
> responses to bullying in the playground or they discuss in detail what clothes they will
> 'wear' in order to fit in with peers. The play is intense and engrossing and is carried on over
> days and weeks in different places.

Many of children's play themes are around difficult and sometimes taboo areas. Vygotsky felt that pretend play develops when children begin to explore some unrealisable desires and tendencies. Imaginary play allows them to explore these within the safety net of the rules developed within the play. You may see here the link to fairy tales and folk tales which seem to develop in all cultures, and where difficult themes are explored (having a step-mother, being orphaned, overcoming evil and so on). In play, the child has moved from exploring things which dictate to the child what he or she must do, to exploring themes or feelings or questions which arise from objects. So a block of wood suddenly becomes a doll; a stick becomes a wand. Through symbolic play the child is learning that language and ideas and objects are not fixed but flexible. Ideas thus allow for *what could be* as well as *what is* and *what has been*. The imagination itself becomes a key feature of development – a central mechanism in communication; something that allows us to explore and respect diversity and to conceive of and create change.

Freud conceived of play as something cathartic for children, allowing them to go into and emerge from reality in order to experience mastery and control. Children could then deal with their own anxieties, fears and conflicts in a safe way. This is the root of many of the play therapies which have since developed. Penny Holland (2003) researched the difficult issue of aggressive behaviour in very young children and looked at what might happen if the nurseries abandoned their 'no tolerance' to gun-play policies. She referred to some of the findings of Dunn and Hughes (2001), who found that children who use violent play themes are less frequently involved in pretend play than children who turn to other themes. They also found that those children who engage in violent play scenarios are more like to show anti-social behaviour at the age of six. It is important to note that they did state that there was no evidence for a claim for a causal relationship. Holland examined what happened in settings where the prevailing ethos of zero tolerance to play with guns was lifted. She looked particularly at the aggressive play of boys. Her contention was that banning play with objects was ineffective at best and damaging at worst. A close examination of what the children are actually playing about and exploring is worth doing.

Paley, who has for many years involved children in dramatic play in her classrooms, is also aware of the fact that many boys in the US are engaged in aggressive behaviour using guns if they are available or making them where they are not. She invites the children to make up and act out stories around issues that concern them and notes what happens. She says: 'boys' play is serious drama, not morbid mischief. Its rhythms and images are often discordant to me, but I must try and make sense of a style that, after all, belongs to half the population of the classroom' (Paley 1984: 12).

Play and creative thinking

Play is important because it is the way in which children are able to use and reflect on their experiences, to represent their ideas and to ask and answer the questions that preoccupy them. Rinaldi (2006) describes children as 'the most avid seekers of meaning and significance' (p. 113) and goes on to consider how, through the behaviour they exhibit and the questions they ask, they show us their developing theories. For her and the educators in Reggio Emilia, the underpinning philosophy is a pedagogy of relationships and listening. We might add to that a pedagogy of watching. Children give evidence of their theories through their actions and their words, and sensitive attention to what they say or do gives adults an insight into their developing concepts. The children are being creative in bringing together what they know and what they have experienced in order to create new understanding. You will remember this from Bruce's notion of play as an integrating mechanism.

Here are some examples drawn from Rinaldi's work:

> Federica, aged three years and two months, wanted to show a running horse in her drawing. She knew that horses have four legs and her solution to the problem she had set herself was to draw a figure of a horse with two legs on one side of the piece of paper and then turn the piece of paper over to draw two legs alone on the other side. She has managed to find a solution – her own unique solution to a problem she has set herself. Here is a child being essentially creative.

> A three-year-old boy was playing with a piece of wire. First he made a bracelet and then put the wire on the back of a chair and let the wire become a horseman riding his horse (the chair). Finally, in the play sequence, the child turned it into a horse's ear.

Rinaldi's analysis of what is happening here is that in each case the child is demonstrating what she describes as *divergent* thinking. What she means by this is that the children are bringing together things that don't normally go together because they have no theoretical framework to determine what is correct. The responses of adults to divergent thinking are often negative, giving children an easy message that thinking like that is not acceptable. Go back to Federica's horse and consider the response made to this by two adults:

> A: Federica, don't you know that a horse has four legs?
> J: What a brilliant idea to draw two legs on one side of the paper and two legs on the other side of the paper. Just like the legs on a real horse.

There is tremendous emphasis on offering children in the nursery schools of Reggio Emilia as many different ways as possible of representing and re-representing their ideas. Much talk has taken place about the these so-called 'hundred languages' of children – a phrase coined to describe the different ways in which children explore ideas, concepts and feelings. Educators in Reggio Emilia feel that in talking of languages they build on Vygotsky's work around language, signs and semiotics. There is, of course, much to be said in favour of children having access to many different ways of expressing their thoughts and ideas, but there is also the very real danger that, once again, a view of the ideal childhood, the ideal learner, is rooted in a Western and capitalist tradition where 'opportunities' and access to resources are vital ingredients in successful learning. We repeat that play is a mode of learning. It is certainly one most children discover for themselves and one that appears in most cultures and over times. But it is not dependent on access to things and is as possible in developing societies as it is in consumerist societies. Children play with what is to hand and children learn from all their experiences. In later chapters we turn our attention to how children learn from such terrible things as being soldiers, or being on the streets, or through work.

Moyles (1998) tells us that play can act as a scaffold for other basic learning. What she means by this is that it allows children to cope with not knowing for long enough to enable them to get to know, it frees them from worrying about 'getting it wrong' and gives them time to build their confidence to try new things. Here is an example:

> Sam is having trouble learning to read. He is only five years old and is a child brimming over with theories of his own. He can remember, in detail, things from years before and has a rich internal life where he plays diverse roles in contexts he delights in inventing. Sometimes in his play he 'pretends' to read – always making clear that he knows that this is not 'real' reading, but that it does not matter because it is all in his invented world. He is dealing with what he cannot yet do by trying it out in pretend mode – safely.

Some theorists are interested in the role of emotion in children's play and creativity. We have already agreed that imagination is vital in pretend play. It allows for one thing to be treated as though it is something else. Russ (1999) believes that emotion or affect (or feeling) is also important. Current thinking suggests that two types of affective processes may operate in play. One is *affect states,* which are described as moods or feelings. When children play aggressively, their feelings or moods may be dictating what and how they play. The other is *affect-laden fantasy,* and that refers to the ideas and images and themes that are imbued with emotion. When children play out things that cause them to feel emotions (death or loneliness or fear or separation), they have selected themes or scripts which are imbued with emotion for them. In much pretend play, both of these creative affective processes may occur and develop.

Play and younger children

Earlier in this chapter we talked about the work of Hutt *et al.* (1989). We will now examine their ideas in more detail, particularly in terms of how they discuss the first stages of play. They encouraged theorists to take play more seriously than they had before, arguing that it is not just something that all children do, but that it is something extremely complex and significant in the development of children. You will remember that epistemic play behaviour involved primarily the search for meaning, involving skill and knowledge acquisition, and Hutt believed it required the presence of adults in order to support, encourage, question and so on. Ludic behaviour was characterised as being more playful and requiring adult involvement only in the sense of adults recognising children's needs. The educator Elinor Goldschmied (1994) studied the play of very young children and introduced the term *heuristic play* to describe what she observed. Children's early play was dominated by the need to put things in and take them out, to fill and empty containers. The child just does these things. Clearly there is some pleasure and satisfaction to be had in doing this. Possibly the actions raise questions in the minds of the children as the children notice what happens and either repeat or change their actions. Goldschmied suggested that the role of adults involved with young children was to provide resources to match these observed needs. Goldschmied was stern in recommending that what the children should be offered to play with should be objects made of anything other than plastic. Her lists include things like collections of corks of different sizes, lengths of chain from fine to medium-sized links; large buttons made of bone; empty tins and jars; baskets of different sizes; wooden clothes pegs and so on. She is famous for having introduced what she called 'treasure baskets' and, in her book, links her thoughts to the words of Bruce Chatwin. In *The Songlines* he wrote:

> When an Aboriginal mother notices the first stirrings of speech in her child, she lets it handle the 'things' of that particular country: leaves, fruit, insects and so forth. The child, at its mother's breast, will toy with the 'thing', talk to it, test its teeth on it, learn its name, repeat its name.

Interestingly, drawing on a culture other than a Western culture, Goldschmied suggested that educators should provide babies with things to explore and that none of the things should be a bought toy, but should be the sorts of everyday objects found in the homes of the children. Interesting too is her advice that adults should not intervene, but should stay attentive but quiet. When she turns her attention to role play she again advocates the use of real things rather than toys to sustain interest and maintain play.

Summing up

Now our twenty-first-century child is seen as being able to make meanings from all the events and experiences she encounters and to make her own personal maps – social, emotional, cognitive and symbolic. She makes meaning and shares meaning through representations. One of the ways in which she brings together her thoughts and questions and experiences is through play, where she is able to explore deeply and over time the things that fascinate, frighten, interest or enchant her. As she plays – free of the risk of 'getting it wrong' – she can both consolidate her ideas and thoughts and sometimes transform them. Her play is based around what is available in her culture. She is making culture and beginning to construct metaphors (thinking about how something is like something else). Situated in a community, she is learning through interaction, playing, watching, listening, being apprenticed and sometimes through teaching her peers. A competent child, indeed.

Questions

- Two themes in this chapter are play and creativity. What do you now understand by these terms and how (if at all) does Developmentally Appropriate Practice (DAP) answer the concerns of some who feel it ignores the reality of the lives of the majority of the world's children?
- What are your views on development that talk of a pedagogy of relationships, listening and watching?
- How do you see children making cultures and beginning to construct metaphor?

Chapter 5

The child as symbol user and symbol weaver

In this chapter we start to look at how the child, having started to use symbols in play, moves into understanding the many complex abstract symbolic systems in his or her world. The abstract symbolic systems we pay most attention to in this chapter are talk, writing, reading and number. We explore other abstract systems in the chapters that follow. We revisit the idea of intersubjectivity to find out more about how children are able to work with others, making and sharing meaning.

> Louis has been learning the multiplication tables. His teacher taught him a trick to work out when the nine times table was correct. He spent an inordinate amount of time trying to find other tricks. This is one of the sums he invented; he showed it to an adult working with him and followed it with the detailed explanation given below.
>
> $5 \times 4 = ?$
> $4/2 = 2$
> $= 20$
>
> Imagine you are doing 5×4. Now 4 is an even number, so for even numbers you break them into half and then add a zero to the number. See?
> Now listen carefully because the odd numbers are harder. Imagine we are doing 5×3. 3 is the number you are going to work on, so this time you go for the number before 3 which is two. Then break it into half which is 1 and add a 5 to it, which makes it 15!
>
> (Figueiredo 1998: 30)

A letter to Sandra from Chloe (an example of the child as symbol user)

What it means to be human

Human beings are the only known species to have developed and used *cultural tools* which, you already know, mean things like traditional tools themselves as well as symbolic systems. So when we talk of cultural tools we could be referring to objects like hammers and computers and magnetic resonance imagers; or to languages and mathematical symbols; or to graphic representations or drawings or maps or paintings and sculptures; or governments and religions. None of these things is the result of the work of one or two individuals. They are collective products of culture created by many individuals and groups over time. You will know that great apes, although genetically close to us, have not developed anything resembling cultural tools. And it is likely that a child born and placed immediately on a desert island with no other people to interact with would almost certainly not be able to invent for herself music, or algebra or an alphabetic system. What makes humans unique, then, is our ability to create culture and the main thing that enables us to do this is something we have already addressed: the ability to understand other people's intentions, to interact with them and to learn from them.

Let us look again at some of the theories about how this happens. Tomasello and Rakoczy (2003) suggest the following:

• At the age of about one year, children understand that other people are intentional agents (which means they are acting with some purpose or goal in mind). They are able to interact with other people and learn from them. This is what we talked of earlier and called *intersubjectivity*. At this very young age children are able to participate in and master some cultural activities, including spoken language. By the age of two, children understand the relationships between self and other and are able to take different perspectives on things. They can reflect on and make some judgements of their own thinking. This is *shared intentionality*.

• At the age of about four, children are able to understand other people (sometimes called 'theory of mind'). This means that the children are able to understand others as mental agents, and this implies that they can appreciate that others have thoughts and beliefs and these are not necessarily always right or correct. Through their interactions with others their understanding becomes more complex and they begin to comprehend some of the cultural institutions rooted in the collective beliefs and values of the culture – things like money systems and marriage and so on. These activities are *collective intentionality*.

• Human beings appear to be unique, also, in being able to understand, consider and reflect on the psychological states of people (how people feel) as demonstrated by one-year-old children understanding such things as intentions and attention. You will remember some of Judy Dunn's finding with regard to this. Tomasello and Rakoczy (ibid.) argue that this is a biological imperative (human beings are impelled to do this) and that what follows – the ability to comprehend communicative systems – requires that children engage with others in social and linguistic interactions with no particular biological underpinnings. Their argument is that the key event, intersubjectivity (what they call the 'real thing') takes place when the child is possibly only one year old.

Babatunde's mother hums as she chops the vegetables. Babatunde (aged 9 months) imitates her by making humming sounds.

In order for this to be possible the child must understand that there are two people involved in this wordless interaction– Babatunde and her mother – and she must understand something of her mother's intention in order to mimic her. When very young children begin to use words to label objects they demonstrate that they understand what words like 'pig' or 'horse' or 'David Beckham' mean. (The choice of nouns here is entirely arbitrary.) Later, children start being selective in the words they use to describe things and they do this to be more precise so that they are more likely to be understood.

Charlie (4:1): That man ... that policeman ... is in his car.

What is happening is that children have worked out that sometimes a word is not enough to accurately portray meaning and they refine what they are saying. Through intersubjectivity they have started to realise that sharing meaning making requires paying attention to whether the listener or the partner in dialogue has actually shared the meaning.

David, talking to his grandmother, was trying to explain a recent experience and he wanted his grandmother to understand exactly what he was trying to say. In a sense he wanted them to have a shared image of what he was describing:

I saw that thingy – you know, that boat ... the blue one ... the canoe.
(David, aged four: personal observation 2001)

Entering the world of linguistic symbols: beginning to talk

From very early on, human infants show a unique communicative pattern of behaviour. They begin to indicate the need to have things labelled or named for them. They do this by looking at or pointing to or holding up objects, inviting others to share attention and provide the label. Tomasello et al. (1999) argue that in this way the child develops the linguistic symbols of his or her culture and moves on to being able to adopt different perspectives at the same time. They reveal an appreciation of the fact that the same person can be a woman or mum or grandma or my teacher, as illustrated by David's explanation here:

That lady over there ... she is my mum and she is my sister's mum too
(David, aged four: personal observation 2001)

Children begin using linguistic symbols (sounds and words, for example) in order to communicate. There is almost certainly some imitation involved as the child repeats words used by adults, internalises the sounds heard and then makes those same sounds in order to make and share meaning. Imitation may be part of the story but there are questions to be asked and answered in order to know whether it, alone, is sufficient.

The first question is what makes it possible to consider talk to be a symbolic act. Often people think of symbols being things that can be seen or touched or held or moved. Talk consists of sounds and these are not random or haphazard but combined in particular ways in order to represent things. Names or nouns represent or stand for objects or people and these are the first linguistic symbols children use. Nouns are then combined with other words in order to create strings of words, phrases and sentences. Language is rule-bound so that the ways in which words can be combined in order to create meaning are clear and are clearly understood by language users. But language is not fixed and static. New words come into languages and some words drop out of languages. You may have seen a recent showing of the programme *49Up* on television and heard a seven-year-old in the year 1963 say 'My heart's desire is to see my father'. This is a phrase almost unknown in the spoken language of today. Not only is language fluid and changing but it is also creative. Children play with language just as they play with objects.

> Sammy, at the age of five, looked at her sister sitting across from her at the table and commented 'She is oppositting me'. She has made a new verb by combining words and concepts – sitting and opposite.

> Two year-old Zac invented the word 'whatbody' drawn from hearing the word 'somebody' and creating its opposite. He asked 'Whatbody gave you that T-shirt?'

> 'Twas brillig, and the slithy toves
> Did gyre and gimble in the wabe;
> All mimsy were the borogroves,
> And the mome raths outgrabe.

The first two examples are of children making up words according to the ways in which they perceive words to work. The third is from that master of playful language, Lewis Carroll, from one of the poems in *Through the Looking-Glass*.

Chukovsky (1963) wrote a fascinating book called *'From Two to Five'*, full of the funny, perceptive and inventive things that Russian children said, revealing their abilities to use language creatively.

The second question relating to how infants learn to communicate is whether the acts that very young children engage in with objects can truly be called symbolic. When a young child puts a doll in a box is the child putting the doll to bed or just putting an object in a container? When the child pushes a block along the ground is the child using the block to represent a car or merely pushing a block along the ground? Tomasello *et al.* (ibid.) believe that many of the examples of symbolic play noted in very young children take place in the presence of adults who scaffold the child's actions. Where adults say to the child something like 'Give the dolly a drink' with a cup and a doll present – objects that are familiar to the child and whose purposes are clear to the child through experience of using them – the child is likely to act out that verbal script. But consider the example of Harris and Kavanaugh (1993) giving the child a yellow block and a teddy and telling the child the teddy is in the bath and asking the child to show them what the teddy does with the soap. It was only children over the age of two who were able to do this because the adults did not model the washing action using the yellow block and also because the children were extremely unlikely to have ever seen anyone washing with a yellow block. Much of the research implies that true symbolic representation only takes place much later than some of the writings suggest.

The third question arises through considering the role of imitation in language acquisition. Language acquisition is a fascinating, tendentious and complex subject and theorists who disagree with one another do so with a passion. The notion that children acquire language largely through imitation dates back to the work of Skinner, some of whose work was touched on earlier in this book. Put very simply, he believed that much of language acquisition came about through imitation and through reinforcement. So the child makes a sound; the adult interprets the sound as meaningful and praises the child; the child repeats the sound. Put crudely the model looks like this:

> The child babbles and within the string of sounds comes something that sounds like 'mama'.
> The mother thinks the child has learned to say the word for mother and kisses the child.
> The praise – the positive reinforcement – makes the child say the word again, hoping for another kiss (or hug or banana).
> The child has learned to say 'mama'.

Using language in order to communicate is a milestone in development. What is fascinating is that this remarkable intellectual feat, which usually takes place within the first year of life, occurs without anyone giving the child lessons. No one sets out to teach the child to talk. Rather, children begin to communicate with other beings through gesture, eye-pointing, expression, intonation and eventually through talk. In this social world children are surrounded by people who use talk in many, many different situations and use talk in order to communicate. The talk children encounter in their homes and communities is talk for real purposes and between people who want to share meaning. There are no tests to fail or trick questions to answer. So the human infant, working hard to understand communication, does so in the supportive company of people who want to communicate with him or her.

The work of Noam Chomsky and his critics

Noam Chomsky (1975), an American thinker and writer, was the first to suggest that language acquisition is genetically determined. He believed that the human infant was born pre-programmed to work out the rules of speech. If you think about it you will realise that speech – in any language – must be rule-governed if people are to be able to use it and be understood. In English, for example, there are rules about the order of words. We can say 'the dog jumped over the fence' but if we say 'the fence jumped over the dog' it makes no sense because a fence cannot jump. If we say 'the jumped fence the over dog' we are uttering a string of exactly the same words but in an order that prevents it from being meaningful. The same rule does not necessarily apply to other languages. In English we have rules about how we use verbs when we talk about the past tense. So we say 'we walked' and 'we talked', the rule being that we add 'ed' to the end of the verb. We have rules about how to talk about more than one object. So we talk about shoes and socks and pens and pencils. The rule here is that we add the letter 's' to the end of a noun to make that noun plural. You, as a fluent speaker of the language, will know that there are exceptions to the rules. We say 'went' instead of 'goed' and 'flew' instead of 'flied'; we talk of sheep instead of sheeps. Chomsky noticed that young children, having started out by saying things correctly through imitating what they heard adults and fluent speakers say, move on to making mistakes by applying the rules to all situations. The way in which he described this was that the children were *over-generalising* the rules. He used this as evidence that children are brilliant thinkers, working out the patterns they hear to make up the rules and then, logically, applying them to all situations.

It was these errors that suggested to Chomsky that children must have something that allows them to use the patterns they hear to work out the rules. What he proposed was that the structure of language, by which he meant the rules that bind it together to make it meaningful, depends on what he called a *language acquisition device* (LAD). You will remember that language has to be rule-bound and the rules known to all for it to be used for sharing meaning. The rules that bind language together are its grammar. The LAD had as its foundation what Chomsky called a *universal grammar* or a linguistic *deep structure* which he believed all humans are born with. The LAD is programmed to recognise, in the surface structure of any natural language (i.e. the words and other features), how the deep structure will operate. So the surface features of the language which are particular to that language (to English, or to Urdu or to Zulu, for example) allow it to be operated by the universal blueprint. This is what accounts for the fact that any human being is born capable of learning to communicate in any language. These are difficult ideas to comprehend and his is an extreme view.

Children are viewed as potentially competent users of language from birth. By competence Chomsky was talking about the underlying and unconscious knowledge of the rule system for generating language that they are born with. The errors or the mistakes children make show us the efforts they are making to find the patterns in the particular language, to work out the rules and apply them. Here are some examples to make this more clear:

Fifteen-month-old Antonio points to the plastic farm animals he is playing with and labels them – 'cows, horses, sheep'.

Here you can see that this very young child is imitating the correct form of plurals he has heard the fluent speakers in his world use. He has not yet worked out the pattern that operates in English for making plurals. One might say that he is 'just copying'.

At three years Antonio points to the plastic sheep and labels them 'sheeps'.

Now the child has moved on from making a grammatically correct response to making an error or a mistake. Chomsky believed that this is because Antonio has been paying attention to what he hears and has worked out that adults have a pattern for making plurals: they add an 's' at the end of the word. Antonio uses this pattern or rule to form all plurals he says. He hasn't yet learned what we know: that there are often exceptions to the rules. The consequence is that he applies the rule to all situations. In the language of Chomsky he overgeneralises the rule. No amount of correction at this stage will enable him to rectify his errors. It is only when he has discovered that there are rules and exceptions to rules that he will be able to use both forms. In other words, only with experience of listening to experienced others will he self-correct.

Steven Pinker (1994) is a linguist who was very influenced by the work of Chomsky and who went on to write about the work of Chomsky in his book *The Language Instinct*. This is a very readable and chatty book, full of amusing games with language, combined with some intricate explanations. The very title of the book points to the view of language acquisition that he shared with Chomsky – that it was genetically determined. Pinker tells us that from Chomsky we learn two things:

1   That language cannot be merely a repertoire or a range of responses since every thing anyone utters or understands is a novel or new combination of words. When a child says 'The birds flied off' or 'I seed it and I feeled it and it's not a dog' each of these is a unique set of words, making meaning, but never before uttered by any human being. So the brain must hold a recipe or a programme or a blueprint that can build an infinite number of sentences out of a finite list of words. These are known as *mental grammars*.

2   That children develop these mental grammars which are very complex extremely rapidly and without formal teaching.

Bruner, whose work you have already encountered, was influenced by the work of Chomsky and saw it as taking a leap forward from previous theories in thinking about how children acquire language. He was very interested in language and particularly in talk. He saw a gap in Chomsky's theory and that gap was the lack of any reference to other people, which means to interaction, to culture or to context. For Bruner the development of language requires at least two people involved in negotiation. The purpose of language is communication and it is through communication that meaning is made and shared and fine-tuned. So, building on Chomsky's LAD, Bruner proposed a more sociocultural model which he called the language acquisition support system (LASS). This he conceived of as a kind of adult scaffolding system. Children learn language through their interactions with others, who cue the children's responses and share meanings with them in particular contexts and within cultures.

Bruner was very interested in the linguistic games and routines that occur between caregivers, particularly mothers, and infants in the early years. He believed that interactions like these were evident in all cultures and that they laid the essential foundations for the development of communicative systems. He identified several ways in which the LASS helps the child move from prelinguistic (before spoken language) to linguistic communication. His focus is on what he calls *formats*, of which he defined three types.

The first formats are the routine and familiar formats where the adult highlights the features of the world that are meaningful for the child and that have a basic or simple grammatical form. By the features he was talking about aspects of the context or the situation. The interactions are often between mother and child and the formats are built around simple games. One of the formats he analysed was the simple 'peekaboo' type of game with which you may be familiar, whereby something or someone is present, then made to 'disappear' and then to reappear, usually accompanied by a verbal noise like 'boo!' Games like this do not occur in the animal world; they occur only in the human world, perhaps because they are dependent on some use and exchange of language. These games provide the child with the first opportunities for systematic linguistic exchanges with an adult and an opportunity to explore how things get done with words. This is Bruner's analysis of what happens:

> The game (something disappears and reappears, accompanied by a sound) has been made up or constructed by people and it follows a set pattern and is tied together with simple rules which can vary only slightly.

The key points are that it is a routine (i.e. follows the same sequence) and that it is rule-bound. In order for the game to work, both players must play it in the routine way.

The fact that there are rules makes it analogous with language in some ways. In addition, Bruner described the game as having both a deep structure and a surface structure. He called the disappearance and reappearance of the object or person the deep structure. The surface structure can be made of changing features, just as the surface structure of language is made up the features of a particular language. So in the game the surface structure could be the cloth under which an object is hidden; or the hands in front of the face. It could also be the variation in the time of suspense involved and the actual words used. So added to the rules are the deep and the surface structures. More than that the game involves turn-taking – an essential element of linguistic exchanges. There is a hider and a seeker; an actor and an experiencer. The game can be seen as a small proto-conversation. The adult does something; the child responds; the adult does something in response to the response and so on. If you have watched a small child engaged in a peekaboo game you will have witnessed the expectation, the anticipation, the revelation and the intense pleasure involved.

The second formats move into spoken language and are where the adult encourages and models lexical (or word) and phrasal substitutes for familiar gestural and vocal means in order to effect different communicative competence. So instead of hiding something and saying 'boo!' the adult might hint, verbally, at a surprise to come: 'one, two, three ... look!' These might include asking questions, giving answers, eliciting information and so on. And as adults play these word games with children they are modelling the different ways in which spoken language is used for different purposes. This is a feature of the way in which the child learns to ask for or request something. One of the things young linguists have to do in order to request something is to share the focus of attention with the adult. Here is a classic example of a word game modelling aspects of questioning: 'I spy with my little eye something that looks good enough to eat', whilst looking at an apple. Looking at something or pointing to something indicates to the child that a shared focus of attention is necessary for communication. Here are two examples to illustrate what children do to share the focus of attention:

> Six-month-old Julie looks intently at her doll which is on a shelf in her room. Her mother follows her gaze and gives her the doll.

> Nine-month-old Julio points to the apple in the fruit bowl and shakes his head when his grandma hands him the banana.

Adults involved with young children are very skilled at showing babies how to do this and use a range of tones of voice, gestures, eye-pointing and other means to share their focus of attention with the child. The child then adopts similar ways of focusing the adult's attention.

The third format is the play format which allows the child to enter a pretend world or an imaginary world in which he or she can adopt different roles and speech forms, address different audiences, and try out new linguistic forms. Here is an example where a group of children are playing hospitals and come in and out of role, changing tone of voice, intonation pattern and style of speaking as they do so:

> Sacha, Stanley, and Holly are playing hospitals in the home corner. They are five years old:
> Sacha: Right, now what seems to be the matter?

Holly: My baby was sick this morning. She went blue in the face and she started crying in a very loud voice. I was worried and so we have brought her here.

Sacha: *Stanley, you be the nurse.*

Stanley: *I can't be a nurse. I am a boy.*

Holly: *Boys can be nurses, you silly. Be the nurse.* Put on that costume.

Stanley obeys and puts on a high-pitched voice. Here baby, What's the matter. (He takes the doll and pokes its stomach.) This baby is very, very, very sick. This baby is going to die. You will be very sad, won't you mommy?

Holly: Oh no! I don't want my baby to die. You are a nurse. Make her better.

Stanley: I am the boss here and I will make her better and then, Mrs Holly, you can take her home and look after her better.

NOTE: The text in italics is when the children come out of role and you can see how they language changes. They are adapting their language to the context and to the roles they are playing. Out of role Holly becomes very bossy.

The work of Michael Halliday: thinking about semiotics

Halliday (1978) looked at language acquisition but from a very different perspective. He was influenced by Eastern European linguists and by British and American anthropological linguists. His approach was fundamentally different to that of Chomsky. He spoke of language *development* rather than language acquisition. This was because he conceived of language as being an infinite, variable and dynamic resource for making and sharing meaning and being constructed and maintained through interaction. You will remember that Chomsky spoke of language acquisition and this term may conjure an image of language as a commodity – something that one can acquire and that is finite, unitary, monolithic and fixed. Used to describe language it suggests that language is something an individual either 'has' or 'lacks'.

Linguists refer to Halliday's view of language as *systemic-functional linguistics* (SLF). Halliday states that the interactions between infant and caregiver in the first six months of life are crucial. During these interactions there is what he calls an 'exchange of attention' which he sees as the beginning of language. There may be no content to this exchange, but it is about feelings and it has meaning. Halliday emphasises two things: that *language is a system for making meaning* and that *meaning is created in the process of mutual exchange.* The communication that develops as the child uses these shared attention contexts for engaging with the real world in these early months is known as *protolanguage.* Exchanges in the first six months are essentially inter-subjective, but once the child starts vocalising or gesturing, the objective domain is introduced So the communication is no longer about feelings and needs alone but comes to be about objects or things. There are a number of projects detailing how children in the second half of the first year of life begin to invent sounds or gestures in order to address others or to draw attention to objects or events. When children are engaged in interactions with other people two things may happen: the focus of attention can be explored *with* them in order to understand it better or *through* them in order to bring about some change. Halliday calls these two ways of engagement the *reflective* and the *active.*

Halliday's work is difficult to understand partly because of his use of very specific language. He suggests that the move from protolanguage to language itself involves the development of a semiotic system. *Semiotics* is often defined as the study of signs and symbols, what they mean and how they are used. You will have encountered signs and symbols and we have already talked about the importance of children developing an understanding of how one thing can stand for or represent another. In language the words we use, the words we say and the words we read are all symbols: they represent aspects of the real world. Marion Whitehead tells us that 'Human verbal language is a systematic and symbolic means of communication' (1997: 13).

Semiotics (this system of signs and symbols) is made up of the following:

- *semantics* (which is meaning in language);
- *syntactics* (which refers to the formal properties of signs and symbols – i.e. grammar); and
- *pragmatics* (which is the study of language in social contexts).

In order for any child to use language effectively the child has to deal both with interpersonal meaning and with representation. Halliday calls representation *ideational meaning*. So the child is having to share meanings and to reflect on or think about meanings. Halliday calls interpersonal meaning and ideational meaning *meta-functions*. They are 'functions' because they comprise the basic uses of language (to interact with another and to make sense of experience). They are 'meta' because they are not within the child but outside of the child and are the way in which meaning has become embedded in the sign or symbol.

Vygotsky and language

Vygotsky was interested in the development of 'higher psychological functions' such as attention and memory. A key feature of these higher functions is that they are mediated by the use of signs. We mentioned this in Chapter 2. Some years ago it was common to tell someone to tie a knot in their handkerchief in order to remember something. The knot acts as a sign or symbol, allowing the person to remember something. It stands for or represents the thing to be remembered. This is important because it transforms remembering from a process dependent on direct stimulation from the environment to a process that can be voluntarily regulated and reflected on. The learner no longer has to be in the presence of the thing to be remembered but has made an internal representation to allow him or her to remember the thing. Nowadays fewer people carry handkerchiefs and people have developed different (and sometimes very personal) ways of creating signs or symbols to enable them to have a mental representation of something. This is what allows us not only to remember, but also to think about the things we remember, so we reflect on what we recall.

Here is an example to illustrate this:

> Four-year-old Joe could remember in detail some of the things that had happened on a visit to his cousin's house in Manchester a year before this conversation took place. He said 'We had a blue car and we stayed in a big house. I was in one room right at the top and my sister was in the room with me. There was a cat and I was scared that the cat would bite me ... or scratch me (giggles). I was only little then.'

You can see how a return visit to his cousin's house prompted Joe not only to remember some of the physical details of an event long past, but also to think back and reflect on his own behaviour. He could remember being scared that the cat would bite or scratch him and analysed that as justifiable because he had been 'only little then'. Talking and thinking about an event and being able to reflect on it through language are complex higher-order cognitive skills.

According to Vygotsky not only were higher psychological functions mediated by the use of signs, but they arose out of social interaction. Vygotsky believed that, in human development, these higher mental functions appear twice: first as *inter-mental* functions which arise through interactions and are mediated by speech, and then as *intra-mental* functions, mediated by internalised semiotic processes. You will have encountered this in Chapter 3. Deconstructing the difficult terminology used, Vygotsky was saying that learning first takes place through interactions between people and specifically in interactions where speech takes place. What happens then is that the child who is a participant in the interaction reflects on what has happened and internalises this, drawing on previous experience and understandings. In other words, children are conscious and mentally active beings from birth, but with the advent of speech, their consciousness is shaped by language. Language, however, can only function in this way as a feature of the individual's (intra-mental) cognition on the basis of having first been initially experienced (inter-mentally) in communicative exchanges with others (Painter 1999: 26). You will already know that Vygotsky's strong focus on the importance of interaction has influenced educators over many years. Children learning collaboratively in groups or pairs; adults scaffolding learning; an awareness that a child's performance can provide a window into the child's potential; and a recognition of the importance of language for learning are all to be observed or understood in many schools and settings.

Vygotsky, as you will realise, was interested in the links between speech and thought. He drew a distinction between pre-intellectual speech (speech before the emergence of thought) and pre-verbal thought (thinking before the emergence of talk). Children, under the age of about two, use vocal activity in interaction to communicate their feelings and emotions and to establish and maintain social contact. They are also capable of goal-directed or purposeful activity which does not require speech.

Here are some examples:

Amina, involved in a peekaboo game with her carer, joins in with the 'boo' by laughing aloud to show her pleasure. (Using vocal activity to join in and show the emotion of pleasure.)

Amina drags a chair over to the shelf near the window of her room and climbs onto it to reach her favourite toy duck. (Goal-directed activity without speech.)

This stage – sometimes described as 'primitive' – is followed by a stage of so-called 'practical intelligence' where the child uses syntax and logical forms of language which have parallels in their problem-solving activities but may not be linked to them in any particularly useful way.

Here is an example to illustrate this:

Liam is drawing on a piece of paper, using a thick blue felt pen. As he draws he chants 'Ooh, a thick blue line. Very nice. Thick and blue. I like blue. It's my best colour. Except for red (changes pen) which is also my best. And gold. I love gold.'

(Using spoken language to parallel what he is doing but not really to reflect on what he is doing or solve any problems he has set himself.)

In the third stage the child starts to use external symbolic means – speech or other cultural tools – to assist internal problem-solving. It is at this stage that we often overhear children talking aloud as they solve problems or describe their actions.

> Mohammed arrives in the nursery and announces that he is going to build a tower from the top down. The teacher is very interested in what he does and watches and records what happens.
>
> Goes to fetch small ladder. Gets Avril to help him set it up.
>
> M: Please put it here, Avril. Just on the carpet so the tower will be right in the middle. Now I need to get some blocks to start the tower. I am going to take two of these big flat ones because they will look really nice at the top. They could be like a helipad.
>
> Picks up two flat blocks, holds them in one hand and climbs up the ladder.
>
> M: Nearly ready now.
>
> Reaches the top – stretch out his hand and stops.
>
> M: Oh, no! It isn't going to work, is it? Because when I let go the blocks won't stay where I want them. They are going to fall. Oh no!

Some authors call this monologuing, and once it becomes internalised Vygotsky called it *inner speech*. The internalisation marks the point when the thinking required for problem-solving has been established. So language becomes something that is used to reflect on action and develop thought rather than as a prerequisite of problem-solving. In other words children become able to use speech and language as tools in their problem-solving because speech allows them to reflect on and consider what they are doing.

The social dimensions of this are apparent as they are in all of Vygotsky's work. The child first expresses emotions and establishes contacts with others and then uses language itself to communicate and to represent thoughts and ideas and this moves on not only to making meaning but to sharing meaning with others. So inner speech moves on to *social speech*. The child's private monologues in the head may be the precursors of thought.

Narrative: language as a dialogic process

Bakhtin (1986) wrote widely about language and had what is often called a *dialogic* view of language. It is not difficult to understand what is meant by dialogic because it is so close to the word dialogue. For him, learning to use language meant learning to interact with others in particular social situations or contexts. Within that context the child learns to be part of an appropriate or dominant 'truth' available within that context. A child coming into a new class, for example, has to learn to be part of the language and the culture of the new class and this involves complex makings of meaning relating to power, control, rules and so on. These are complex ideas, couched in difficult language, but keep reading. What Bakhtin said is interesting and relevant. Let us look at some examples:

> Helena enters a new class in the infants school and finds she is the only black child in the class.

Dominique wants to join the football team but it is made up entirely of boys.

Marlena has just arrived from Poland and has to start school. She is the only Polish speaker in the whole school.

For each of these children you might consider how the child's social positioning might affect what happens. Children's scripts are formed where their social interactions meet their inner meanings and the cultural symbols available to them. The cultural meanings available to a small child will be different from those of a black person or those of a speaker of another language. This means that children learn to talk (and to act) differently in different contexts and with different people. To make this clear you only have to think about how you speak differently at work from the way you do at home; or to your grandparents as opposed to your children; or to friends as compared with powerful others like doctors or lawyers.

According to Bakhtin each individual has a unique point of view. But we live in a world of others and we experience our own perspective – our own understanding of the world – in dialogue with these others. They, in turn, see us as situated in a context. Bakhtin goes on to say that these others become the central figures – the heroes, if you like – of our lives and in the stories we make to explain our lives.

> It is about the others that all the stories have been composed, all the books have been written, all the tears have been shed ... so that my own memory of objects, of the world, and of life could also become an artistic memory.
>
> (Bakhtin 1981: 111–112)

Bakhtin, with his sociocultural approach to learning, offers us a useful framework when we turn our attention to children as story composers, storytellers and narrators.

Stories form one of the cultural tools that are found in every culture we can think of. The members of cultural groups make up and tell and re-tell stories about their lives and their feelings, their experiences and fears, their past and their imagined future. In some cultures – often described as having an oral tradition – stories are passed on through routines and rituals and become changed in the hearing and in the telling. You may well have come across some of the devices storytellers in some cultures have for indicating a story is about to begin: 'Cric-Crac' or 'Are you sitting comfortably? Then I'll begin' are signals to the listeners that a story is to be told; they are cultural narrative markers. In other cultures children hear and see stories on television and videos and in film or in cartoons and books. Children throughout the world begin, from very early on, to structure their own narratives. In order to make meaning and to share meaning children begin to sequence and structure the things they have done or experienced, first into simple protonarratives, but later into more and more complex sequences.

Here is a simple protonarrative told by 22-month-old Hannah when she came across a huge jacaranda tree in the park: 'I could climb up and up and up ... and then down and down and down.' This small child drew on her experience which included knowing the story of 'Jack and the Beanstalk' really well. Whitehead (1997) cites examples of some simple narratives created by children as young as two years old. Here is a wonderful example of what a black two-year-old in the US contributed after a first visit to church:

It's a church bell
Ringin'
Dey singin'
Ringin'
You hear it?
I hear it
Far
Now

(Heath 1983: 1700)

This child is using poetic language (the arrangement of the words on the page is that of an adult, of course). What is significant is the act of composing or making up a story which appears to be an essential ingredient of development. It involves selecting and structuring experience and feelings into something that can be told and listened to and reflected on. Harold Rosen, in a pamphlet produced for the National Association for the Teaching of English and called *Stories and Meanings* (1984), tells us that there may well be a disposition or a tendency to narrative that is as universal as (or more so than) Chomsky's universal grammar. Barbara Hardy (1968) calls storying a primary act of mind. Bruner, too, regarded narrative as a primary meaning-making tool. It appears that there may be a universal desire to create stories and the making of stories requires exposure to the cultural ways of storying we encounter. There is no correct way of making stories: we learn the story grammars and discourses and patterns from our society and our culture.

Rosen reminds us that it is important, however, to remember that narrative is fiction. Story makers – children and adults – draw on their own experience but also use their imagination: the worlds in their heads. So we are back to the words of Bakhtin about using others as our heroes. As story composers we cannot remember everything. We have to select the salient features of the story we want to tell and we use language as a means to order experiences and memories. Rosen tells us that the story is out there, somewhere, awaiting a crucial step. The creator of the story must seek for and make meaning. To give order then to all the possible ways of telling that story a sequence must be plotted; we must invent beginnings and ends. In each story there must be a resolution or an outcome. Contradictions must be resolved. A tale must be told.

There is a long tradition in Jewish literature ... of bearing witness through telling stories ... In this way, history is preserved as personal history; history is given shape and meaning through the interpretation of individual lives. And just as history is made up of personal histories so too are personal identities formed in relation to a larger ethical and cultural context.

(Aarons 1996: 60)

Understanding that symbols make text: the symbols children use in their spontaneous writing

Much has been written about how children come to understand the written world in which they live. Researchers have looked at how very young children attempt to write and in doing so invent or re-create the symbols of their culture and language. At the beginning of this chapter is a letter from Chloe to Sandra. This is an example of a very early piece of writing. Chloe used coloured felt pens and made zigzag marks across the page – one line for each colour. As she made the marks she related a simple 'story' to her mother. As she did this she revealed some of her thinking about what it is that writers do.

One of the most significant early pieces of work was a study of how children come to construct their own hypotheses about print and the alphabetic system. Ferreiro and Teberosky's seminal work *Literacy Before Schooling* (1983) describes a project examining the hypotheses of four- to six-year-old Spanish-speaking children from differing socioeconomic backgrounds. The children were asked to produce disconnected fragments of writing in somewhat formal conditions, in a one-to-one relationship with an adult rather than in their peer groups. Tasks tended to focus on the *orthographic* features of the words. These are the marks that children make in their attempts to write. The findings are interesting and sometimes moving. They are often surprising. Ferreiro and Teberosky found, amongst other things, that four-year-old children know what makes a picture and what makes 'writing'; they know that writing is more than just squiggles, lines and dots, but symbols representing something else; they do not know that writing is 'speech written down'. Something that is large in life (an elephant, perhaps) is represented by them by a symbol or group of symbols of proportionate size. Names of objects or people are the only linguistic forms to appear in the writing of these children. Ferreiro and Teberosky arrived at a stage theory of development in writing as children move on from their previous hypothesis when something occurs to cause some cognitive dissonance. Here is an example:

> Sukvinder wrote a series of parallel straight lines and said it was writing. Two days later she did the same thing, but this time included some dots and curly lines. A week later she said 'I've got too many of these all the same ones'.

Ferreiro and Teberosky proposed that children naturally, over time, go through a predictable sequence from early mark-making to more recognisable letter-like forms and then on to alphabetic letters which are finally linked to sounds. There are studies which show that children make a similar journey whatever language they are attempting to write.

Significant as this study was at the time, there was little opportunity for children to display a repertoire of skills in terms of the kinds of symbols they might use in varying contexts. Sulzby (1986) showed that the requests of adults affected the symbols children used. Children asked to write everything they could tended to write lists of words using conventional spelling, but when asked to write like grown-ups they produced scribble – showing an awareness of the shapes of cursive scripts. Marie Clay, working in New Zealand in 1993, observed five-year-old children in classrooms and she found something different. Rather than a clear linear progression she found that children, once they started to write, used a mix of principles. For example, they began to realise that a limited number of signs is required (Sukvinder in the example above shows a dawning realisation that too much repetition is not acceptable as 'writing'); and that a limited number of signs when used in different combinations will result in different words (for example rat, tar, art are all made up of the same three letters). This is a clear focus on signs: Clay's approach is *semiotically* based. The children pay attention to writing as a system of signs in which how the features are arranged is vital. They pay attention to features like how the marks are aligned on the page, to the direction in which they are written and read, and to the specific aspects of the written language they see in their homes and cultures. Bengali children sometimes include horizontal lines in their early writing and Urdu or Arabic early writers used many curls and dots.

Vygotsky focused, too, on semiotics and he did not see the development of writing as linear, but rather as a complex and dialectical process where children go backwards and forwards, using changes and transformations. Early writing, characterised by simple mark-making, appears to disappear only to re-appear later on in a different form. So he saw children's development as writers as social, dynamic and continuous. The child's understanding of signs is interwoven with sociocultural experience and you will remember reading earlier in this book how language is used to construct and mediate interactions and how there is constant interplay between the interpersonal (what happens inside the child's thinking) and the intrapersonal (what happens between the child and others).

So now the children, as symbol users, relate the forms of the signs and symbols to the various discourses (or genres) they encounter. Harste *et al.* (1984) found that children as young as five were able to use different types of symbols to depict different genres: they could make maps and lists and personal letters. Some children in nursery classes have been seen to write 'a song' using musical notation. Kress (1997) has observed that children will use whatever is to hand to make representations of things.

> Abdul, aged seven, made a model of a moving creature based on something he had seen on television; then he drew the creature and then made one out of Meccano. Finally he produced a small collection of drawings with labels on which he called a 'Meccano catalogue'.

Kress states that children develop a social semiotic way of representation and communication and they choose signs and symbols that are best suited to their intentions. He identifies two principles to explain the choices children make. One is *interest* which arises from where the child is and what the child finds of interest, and allows the child to make his or her own individual representation. The other principle is *metaphor* which suggests the most appropriate things to use for the representation. The question the child appears to ask here, in the choice of resources to use, is 'What is most like this thing I want to represent?' You can see how analogy comes into play here.

When children come to use symbols to create text they are trying to represent ideas that are important to them. Barrs (1988) cites the wonderful example of a five-year-old boy who made a map to be used with a complex play sequence where a hero figure had to overcome physical obstacles. The child placed symbols on his map to give instructions to an adult who had to play the role of the hero.

Below is an example of a very young child's early attempts at writing her name. Her mother has put circles around each of the three attempts and added an explanation to help know what the child was doing. In the first attempt the child wrote from right to left and said that it was her name, Chloe. In the second attempt she wrote from left to right and there is a clear one-to-one correspondence between the letter-like shapes and the letters in her name. In the final attempt she wrote from top to bottom. It is apparent that she knows that her name includes one letter that looks like a vertical line and one that looks like a circle and she includes the letter C in one attempt. What is apparent is how hard she is working to 'write like a writer'. She was not yet three years old.

Into the world of reading

We clearly do not have room in this book to discuss in any great detail how children become readers. As you will know this is an area even more contentious than some of the other issues we have looked at. However, in light of our contention that children actively seek to make and share meaning, we can focus on how children, in their encounters with the written world, seek to make sense of it and of what the others in their world do with it. Children seek to understand what it is that readers do when they see marks on a page, on an advert, on a road sign and so on. So becoming a reader also becomes a sociocultural event with expert readers mediating what happens between the child and the symbols on the page (or on the hoarding or on the sign or wherever).

Infants will explore books just as they explore other objects they encounter. Many books encourage exploration through the use of colour, picture, and devices like flaps to be lifted, holes to be peeked through and so on. The books designed like this operate on the assumption that children will be encouraged to explore the books alone, or with others, and will use some of the routine built into games like the peekaboo games discussed earlier. The 'lift the flap' books relate very obviously to the peekaboo games. Children who are fortunate enough to be able to engage with books together with adults may have their introduction to book-reading take place in positive exchanges. Since books read to a child sometimes allow the child to explore some painful issues safely, this emotional support can be very helpful. This is not to imply that those who come to books later or through their own will not become and remain readers.

When children start to read they may start by re-telling the story, first from the pictures or from their memory of what the story is about. From there they move on to paying attention to the actual marks on the page, realising that it is these marks that make the story remain the same on each re-reading. In the ideal case, children are seeking to find the meaning, to lift the writer's tune from the page, as Myra Barrs tells us. Sometimes these attempts are frustrated when children are taught at a very young age to pay attention to the units that make up the words that make up the sentences that make up the meaning. So children are taught to pay attention to the smallest units of meaning rather than to the meaning per se. This is the so-called phonics approach to reading.

At some stage apprentice readers do need to learn about the sounds and letters that make up words, and about the rules that make written language readable. Ideally, young readers need to acquire as many strategies or tools as possible to enable them both to decode and to remain engaged in the meaning of what they are reading.

And what are these symbols? Into the language of counting

Marks representing a numeric symbol are found in almost all known cultures. Young children encounter these symbols in many places and begin to consider what they represent. In many cultures children are taught to chant the number sequence often before they have any clear understanding of what it is they are saying. Parents and carers count as children climb up the stairs, or as a child is tossed in the air or as the spoon approaches the open mouth. The question arises as to how the child knows that the words 'one, two, three' and so on are words specifically relating to counting. Gelman (1990) suggests that very young children keep the set of count words separate from their set of labels. This, again, is complicated. Let us take the example of cars. The child, when acquiring speech, learns to attach the label 'car' to vehicles with wheels. They may be blue or green, big or small, but they share some key features. But when the child is presented with four cars and asked to count them the child will not get far simply chanting 'car, car, car, car'. The child needs different labels to do this and these are the labels the language uses for counting – in English, for example, one, two, three, four.

When children come to exploring symbols they will sometimes invent their own symbols to represent a number of objects. One of the most famous studies of this was carried out by Bialystok (1991) who presented children with boxes, each filled with a different number of small objects. She asked the children to stick something on the lid of each box so that they would know how many were in the box without having to lift the lid. Children produced either traditional number symbols or analogical representations (e.g. six dots or six lines or drawings). Analogical notations were less help to the children when it came to recognising and decoding their meaning.

Shown below are four small drawings made by a child to illustrate the four objects in one box. The child had more difficulty in remembering the number and had to count the drawings each time. She was perfectly able to recognise the symbol 4 and to state immediately that there were four objects on the box with this on the lid. Karmiloff-Smith (1992) suggests that this occurs later in development than more simple symbol memory or pictorial representation.

You will realise that numerals are only a small part of coming to understand the world of mathematics, which is in itself an abstract and largely symbolic world. We will talk more about this in the chapter on the child as investigator.

Summing up

In this chapter we have looked at the child as a symbol user and examined the whole concept of symbolic representation, looking at how the child begins to use one thing to represent another and then moves on to more abstract symbolic systems – specifically talk, mark-making, reading and using numerals. The work of Chomsky has been introduced and criticised in light of the views of theorists such as Bruner, Halliday, Bakhtin and Vygotsky. Our twenty-first-century child is now seen to be able to use one thing to represent another and in doing this enters the world of signs and symbols to make and share meaning.

Questions

- This chapter moves into the world of signs, symbols and abstractions. What are your views on the importance of cultural tools in development?
- Daniel Barenboim recently bemoaned the lack of attention in our culture paid to the ear as opposed to the eye in terms of learning and development? What do you feel about this?

Chapter 6

The child in culture

Having spent some time thinking about the child in society and the child beginning to use symbols we now turn our attention to the child in culture and exploring culture. So we look at how children are inducted into their culture and how they define themselves and are defined by others. This introduces the theme of self-identity which we explore in more depth in the following chapter. We also touch on a consideration of the capacities children have to make informed choices within their cultural contexts.

> Luigi is seven years old. He lives in a small village in a relatively unspoiled region of Italy where his mother is part of a group of people who cook together and then set up tables in the streets where friends, neighbours and the odd visitors can come and eat delicious food. He is described by his family as 'the best pasta maker' in the village and they say this is because when he comes home from school he joins the cooks and spends all his time making pasta. They call it his job. At school his teacher describes him as a 'very pleasant but rather slow child with no particular aptitude'.

> Abdul is nine years old. He lives in Baikur. He was asked about what work he does to help his family income and he said that he felt that he can now be involved in watering the plants. He said 'Now that I am nine I am strong enough to carry the water from the well. Last year I was too small and weak. Now I have strong hands and good legs. I water our rice field and our garden for two hours every day. I would like to work in the hotel because you get more money but my parents say I am too young. I go to school in the mornings and when I come home I help with the rice fields and the garden.

We have talked about culture throughout this book without stopping to define it. This is partly because everyone holds a common-sense definition of culture in their heads. This relates to the beliefs, the artefacts, the values, and other things that bind people together. It refers to the music and the food and the language(s) and the religion and the customs and the clothing that make members of a group feel a sense of belonging to that group. This is rather a superficial definition and ignores the role played by the players in making culture and passing it on and changing it. It makes it seem that culture is something fixed and 'given' to those born into it, rather than seeing its dynamic nature. In this sense you can see how close it is to language. Pinker (2002: 60) offers an interesting definition of culture:

> The phenomena we call 'culture' arise as people pool and accumulate their discoveries and as they institute conventions to coordinate their labours and adjudicate their conflicts. When groups of people separated by time and geography accumulate different discoveries and conventions we use the plural and call them cultures.

Cultural tools, as you know, are the artefacts, symbols and systems developed by people within groups and used to make, share and transform meanings. As we said in Chapter 3, cultural tools are often specific to cultures and often used to define culture. You have only to think about how we talk about Chinese food, Italian cars, French style, Yiddish chutzpah or English sense of fair play to see how we take single aspects of one culture and use these to create stereotypes. It does not take much imagination to make the next link to 'Muslim fundamentalism', 'black athletic prowess' or the 'superiority of the English language' to see how dangerous this is. You will not be surprised that all three of these phrases occurred in the English press during one week in September 2005.

Stuart Hall (1992) described how children can be defined by others – often negatively – on the basis of their class, their gender, their race or their language. As children begin to work out who they are (their self-identity) they also try to work out who they are similar to and different from in some ways. So when we identify ourselves as one thing we, at the same time, differentiate ourselves from others who are different in some way. So when we say we are women, we indicate that we are not men, for example. There are also within-group variations. A person who has been an immigrant in this country for a long time will have had different experiences and hence a different identity from a newer arrival although we often tend to talk of them as 'immigrants' as if this gives a clear description of them and their experiences.

Children construct their identities from their experiences and through their interactions. This includes seeing themselves as part of a group sharing a culture. The ways in which they and other members of their group are represented will be crucial in doing this. So children construct their identities partially from how they (the group) are represented. It will feel very different being the only black child in an all-white class, or being the only girl on the football team, for example. How children define and identify themselves is a complex process and one which essentially involves children's self-esteem. The reactions of others to them or to their group impact on self-image and hence on self-identity. Children who encounter few images or predominantly negative images of themselves and their group will suffer damage to their self-esteem and the whole process of identity construction will be difficult.

In Skutnabb-Kangas and Cummins' (1988) book *Minority Education: From Shame to Struggle,* Antti Jalava wrote a piece called 'Nobody could see that I was a Finn'. In this disturbing autobiographical piece he wrote about his experiences after his family moved from Finland to Stockholm when he was nine years old. On the first day at school the principal did not know what to do with this little stranger: all she could do was hold the child's hand as they walked to the classroom: 'Holding hands was the only language we had in common'.

In class the child was called names and teased. He tried to adjust:

> Adjusting was not, however, at all simple. To what did one have to adjust and how? There was nobody to explain things, there were no interpreters, no Finnish teachers and no kind of teaching of the Swedish language. And I was no chameleon, either, for I only wanted to

be myself, out of habit and instinct. <u>When the others wrote in Swedish, I wrote in Finnish</u>. (Smidt's underlining.) But that was something that just couldn't be. The teacher grabbed my pencil and angrily shook his finger at me. In spite of everything I continued to fall back on my mother tongue.

When you read this you get a really strong sense of the child's struggle to both become part of the new host culture (Sweden and school) but also to retain part of his self-identity (his language). In the underlined sentence this is powerfully illustrated. As the children in the class wrote in Swedish Antti did the only thing that was possible for a child who clearly had the capacity to understand the task together with the implied rules and conventions, but was not equipped with the tool of knowing the Swedish language – which proved to be an essential tool.

Antti ended up in the office of the principal and that night threw a stone through the window of the principal's office and never again wrote in Finnish. He bonded with a band of 'brothers' and said that violence became the only language understood by all of them. By the time he moved up to the junior grades he had learned some Stockholm slang and said that the language of the classroom, which he described as middle-class Swedish, was as impenetrable to the working-class Swedish boys as it was to him. He was fiercely homesick and went down to the docks to watch the boats from Finland come and go. He wept in private. But with time the idea grew within him that it was shameful to be a Finn. The way in which he writes about this is powerful and painful:

> "Everything I had held dear and self-evident had to be destroyed. An inner struggle began, a state of crisis of long duration. I had trouble sleeping. I could not look people in the eye, my voice broke down into a whisper, I could no longer trust anybody. My mother tongue was worthless – this I realised at last; on the contrary it made me the butt of abuse and ridicule.
>
> So down with the Finnish language! I spat on myself, gradually committed <u>internal suicide</u> (Smidt's underlining) ... I resolved to learn Swedish letter perfect so nobody could guess who I was or where I came from.

You can see how difference and prejudice can operate against groups and also within groups. This child made the terrible decision to give up his language and become as perfect in Swedish as it was possible to be, precisely in order to disguise his true identity as an individual and his identity as part of a group. The underlined words in the above excerpt illustrate the depths of his despair.

Throughout this book we have been looking at the developing child as more than a constructor of meaning: we have been looking at the child as active, strong, competent and in interaction with others in a range of contexts and settings. Each of these contexts has its own set of beliefs and values – its own set of cultural tools. Children, from their first explorations of the world, interact with, contribute to, adopt and change these beliefs and values as they become members of different cultural groups.

Children's capacities

Writers and theorists are beginning to think in more depth about children's capacities which is, in effect, thinking about their competence to make decisions about issues that affect their lives. There is a general acceptance that adults are competent and children are lacking in competence. This relates to the views of both children and adults. These views are particularly prevalent in the Western world where children are generally excluded from the responsibilities of the adult world, keeping them apart from participation in activities that confer social status. In these societies children are still perceived of as physically, socially, emotionally and economically dependent. Children spend longer and longer time at school and live in this protected cocoon of 'being a child'.

Yet children in many countries are critical of the fact that adults do not acknowledge the responsibilities they take and they recognise that adults often fear that children might become a more vocal and powerful group. Mayall (2000) talked to children between the ages of nine and twelve and these children talked of teachers who offered double standards, by expecting much responsibility and a lot of work at school, while treating the children as unreliable, and lacking in a sense of moral agency. Children said that teachers often accused them of being deceitful or of lying. Some of the children also noted that the independence and respect they sometimes gained at home through being responsible and helpful did not transfer to how they were viewed by teachers. Children are concerned with the levels of respect accorded them in their different cultures. Many adolescent boys feel that they receive no respect at school but can earn respect on the streets through their adoption of the culture of the streets.

Bissell (2002) carried out a piece of research in Bangladesh examining the perceptions children had of themselves and she found that they might describe themselves as either big or small, not on the basis of the physical stature or the wealth of their families but in terms of their own autonomy. One example was of an eleven-year-old girl who described herself as small and explained that that was because she could not make any decisions, nor did she do any work. It emerged that she did, in fact, work in the garment factory, but her self-esteem remained low because she earned less than her parents. In her terms that made her remain 'small'. Another girl talked about how her image varied from medium to small according to whether her mother was away from home or present at home. When her mother was away she was expected to make decisions and carry some of the responsibility for the family. This made her medium, but when her mother returned she reverted to being small. In school she saw herself as small because, she said, 'I don't know anything' (Lansdowne 2005).

Social and cultural expectations clearly play a vital role in the demands made of children – of boys and girls, of younger and older children. This clearly affects the children's capacities to exercise responsibility. In Nepal, girls take on the adult work roles at the age of twelve, whilst boys do not do this until two years later. Indian girls are perceived to reach adulthood at the age of fourteen years whilst boys do not attain this until they are sixteen. In Bangladesh, children are perceived to cross a threshold that separates out a stage of innocence (*shishu*) from an age of knowing. This transition is not associated with specific ages. Tonga children of both sexes in Zimbabwe participate fully in the money-earning enterprises of the family from the age of ten. It is clear from this that children make sense of how they are perceived by others in their cultural contexts and often recognise that they are sometimes perceived as not being capable when, in essence, they are.

Some interesting work demonstrating the capacities of children with disabilities is being carried out through the auspices of Save the Children UK, which has set up a project in Neap where 22 children with disabilities who have been successful in getting some education in mainstream schools are being encouraged to tell their stories about their successes to other children with disabilities. A famous Nepali writer has worked with the children and helped them get their studies published in newspapers. This raises the profile of disability, offers role models and allows children to raise their expectations of what they can achieve.

The intersecting cultures of childhood

Bronfennbrenner (1979) was one of the first theorists to examine the intersecting worlds of children through his 'ecological' model. This model is often represented as a set of concentric circles, one within the other, to show the movement from the most intimate contexts of the home to the more remote contexts beyond. So the innermost circle, the *microsystem*, represents the everyday context of the life of young children, which is usually the home but may move beyond into the extended family, the neighbourhood and perhaps the crèche or the nursery setting. The next circle represents what are known as the *mesosystems* and these are seen to be the links between home and clinic, home and church or mosque or synagogue, between home and nursery or school and so on. More remote yet are things that affect the child more indirectly and these are called the *exosystems*, and include things like community networks and the workplace of the parents, perhaps. Finally, and most remote from the child but still impacting on his or her life, are the *macrosystems*, which are where social systems like laws and economics and the media and the education system make decisions that affect the child and his or her family. You can see how the child's cultures come together through this model.

Within each of their cultural groups children set about defining themselves as members of that group, using the cultural tools available to them to define their family roles, their gender roles, their images, their languages, their complex worlds. This, the construction of identity, is one of the earliest tasks for the human infant. Neither identity nor culture is fixed but they are dynamic and fluid and can be considered as relational and relative concepts. So the identity of the child at home is not one thing but can be *baby* or *sibling* or *competent* or *difficult* according to circumstance and context. Here are some examples:

> Masha is very quiet and withdrawn when her Uncle Leo visits. He is a big and noisy man and he terrifies her. But when he leaves she returns to being her cheerful and outgoing self.

> Henry is the older sibling and is expected to be grownup and sensible and responsible. Usually he is but every so often he loses his temper and resorts to stamping his feet and shrieking like a two-year-old.

The identity of the child away from home requires further construction and elaboration. We know that in order to construct self-images in new contexts the child has to come to know which cultural tools are available and use these in order to become part of that context. We would suggest that children need to make sense of a wide range of things like language(s) including dialects and registers; discourse(s) or ways of speaking and acting; religious practices and belief systems; values and norms including knowing what is acceptable and what not; and customs, which can include ways of eating and dressing and speaking and interacting and learning. So within their separate and their intersecting cultures children learn the relevant tools and sometimes encounter conflicts and dichotomies. We have seen this earlier in this chapter and will meet further examples of the dissonance that can be created where there is some conflict.

Cultural capital: the ideas of Bourdieu

Bourdieu was a Marxist sociologist who examined aspects of society in terms of things like power and class. In Marxist theory capital is power which is acquired through labour or work. If you work and earn a salary that salary is your capital and you can use it to acquire more capital in terms of a place to live, possessions and so on. It is capital which forms the foundation of the class system and social structure in many societies. Bourdieu believed that capital should also have a symbolic component – so that it went beyond the economic definition. By symbolic capital he meant things like cultural, social and linguistic facts which can either benefit individuals or hold them back. Like that of many theorists, his writing is difficult to understand because of the dense language he used. We will take time to define some of the terms he used.

- *Cultural capital* can be loosely defined as being 'what people know'. Perhaps you are studying for a qualification and when you have completed your studies part of your cultural capital will be what you have learned.
- *Fields* are things like 'from home to school' or places where things take place, or exchanges are held.
- *Social capital* can loosely be defined as 'who people know'. You will be familiar with name-dropping – the habit of inserting the names of famous people or current celebrities into conversation in order to impress people. The people you know may well contribute to your social capital.
- *Habitus* is a system of dispositions or habits or attitudes which explain the differences we see in all societies between and within groups. Put crudely, children with a disposition to enjoy formal education and learning are more likely to succeed in schooling. Habitus is acquired by individuals and by groups through experience and is the product of the history of the family or individual and of their class and cultural context. Within the concept of habitus there is the concept of *family habitus*. The family habitus of middle-class children in the United Kingdom is likely to be closer to the habitus valued and recognised by teachers.

You will realise that Bourdieu's use of the concept of cultural capital was a *social and cultural* analysis of the reasons for the failure of individuals and groups. It situated the reasons within an economic and power framework and specifically stated that failure was not the result of a lack of natural aptitude. In other words, certain groups of children may struggle at school because of the effects of poverty or the impact of prejudice, not because of lack of ability. Aspects of the notion of cultural capital have been criticised as offering a rather passive view of the child in their acquisition of capital and some of this relates to the emphasis in some of the studies on how mothers and other caregivers are viewed as being able to 'give' their children the necessary cultural capital to allow them to succeed as learners. This is an attempt to explain why in many places poor children fail to thrive in the educational systems. Bourdieu is an important thinker and writer who has contributed much to our understanding of children and culture. Prout (2005), however, reminds us that Bourdieu's theories do not fully allow for children being active agents in

their acquisition of capital and in their abilities not only to appropriate but also to transform culture.

Children inhabit complex cultural worlds and to each new field or context children
bring a store of cultural capital. You will realise that where the cultural capital children
bring is close to that valued and held by an institution (for example the classroom), children are likely to be advantaged. Their cultural capital is accessible to their educators.
Where children bring cultural capital that is divergent from that of their educators, the
educators do not know what to recognise and value. The habitus of 'now' is the sum
total of the culture and class history of the individual and family.

In the school attended by Hannah and Ben the family habitus they bring is different from
that of many of their peers. Since many of the pupils are members of dominated groups
by virtue of poverty, immigration, ethnic origin, or low occupational classification, they may
share common characteristics in terms of both their responses to their present situations
and also to their hopes and aspirations. It is evident, however, that individuals from dominated groups have become extremely creative and successful in their learning, their lives
and their relations. This is an illustration of the fact that there is a difference in how members of these groups are able to exercise agency and change the aspirations of the family
or group. Each child coming into the classroom brings with her or him the family habitus
but also the potential to develop their own, unique primary habitus. They do this through
the strategies they develop to deal with their own experiences in the context of both the
family habitus and the school habitus. For the novice to schooling whole new sets of rules
and roles and identities need to be mastered in order to become a member of the new
cultures of the classroom, of the dinner hall, of the playground.

Children in the classroom and in the playground start to use their own habitus and their
cultural capital to create new cultures with new rules, roles and identities. When Hannah
first started school the cultural capital she brought included an intimate knowledge of stories in books and from videos. One of the ways in which she worked to use this cultural
capital to become part of a new culture was to 'play' the stories that she knew. This seemingly simple act is, in fact, an extremely complex exploration of cultural meanings. In a
group of children, each with a unique habitus, some agreement must be reached in order
that the children can inhabit a shared imaginary world. Each child has to have an identity
and a place within the story and in order to do that the children need to explore their
own understandings, many of which will be drawn from their personal exposure to culture
– popular and other. Hannah, now aged seven, still takes the stories she reads at home and
sometimes becomes what might be called a 'cultural leader' in that she offers the stories
to her group for them to play. Most recently she has taken in a story she has been reading
with her mother called 'Parvana's Journey' by Deborah Ellis, which is a harrowing account
of the experiences of a young girl in Afghanistan under the Taliban regime. When talking
about the play Hannah commented that one of the children in the group had 'loved the
bit where the hands were cut off'. This exploration of extreme physical aggression and
unfamiliar notions of justice falls into what Dyson calls 'unpopular play' – play which is or
contains elements that adults may not approve of or find suitable. As in the children
described in Dyson's study, the children in Hannah's peer group, creating their playground
culture, are exploring complex issues relating to the real world in which they live and
where they hear, daily, talk of war and weapons. In London in 2003 there is little possibility

for these children, in Year 2, to build on this intense exploration of serious and deeply frightening concerns within the classroom. They spend their days practising for the coming SATS tests. The children demonstrate their skills as creators of culture by doing so in the playground.

(Smidt 2004: 81–82)

As these children play the roles they have agreed on, using their own attitudes and dispositions, they begin to create a new culture – a shared culture brought about by the mixing of their languages, their ideas, their feelings and their experiences.

Languages and culture

Millions of children throughout the world are speakers of more than one language and many of them have come to understand and use the symbolic systems of these different languages. Some recent studies fall into a paradigm based on *syncretism* which was a term used by anthropologists studying how African and European Christian religious traditions overlap and intersect in some Caribbean cultures. Gregory *et al.* (2004) tell us that the term has taken on broader and more positive connotations and has now come to mean the *creative transformation of culture.* To elaborate this we need to examine how syncretic studies sees development as a creative process wherein people, including children, reinvent culture, drawing on their resources, old and new. And since it refers to cross-cultural exchanges, the issue of power is one that has to be considered in the contradictions and sometimes the conflicts that arise. We spoke of the possible conflicts children encounter where there are collisions of culture. Speakers of languages other than English going to school in England clearly have to deal with the host and dominant language (the language of power, of education, of government and of the media) and to find ways of being able to maintain and use their home languages. As we saw earlier in the story of Antti this is one potential area for dissonance.

In summary the principles of a syncretic approach include the following:

1   Children are members of different cultural and linguistic groups and actively seek to belong to these groups in a way which is not linear but is dynamic, fluid and changing.
2   Children do not remain in the separate worlds defined by their cultural group, but move between worlds. According to Kenner (2000) they live in 'simultaneous' worlds. So a child is a member of the cultural group of her family but also is actively creating the cultural group of her setting or classroom. This has echoes of the views of Bronfennbrenner but situates the child as active creator and transformer of culture.
3   As children are members of different groups they syncretise or transform the languages and narrative styles, the role relationships and learning styles appropriate to each group and then transform the cultures and languages they use to create new forms. We have seen examples of this in previous sections.
4   Children who are fortunate enough to interact in cross-linguistic (where more than one language is involved) and cross-cultural (where more than one culture is involved) practices are able to call on a wider range of *metacognitive* and *metalinguistic* strategies. These terms need defining. Metacognitive means the ability to think

about thinking itself; metalinguistic means knowledge about language itself. These strategies are further enhanced when the children are able to play out different roles, which we will look at in the next chapter.

5   All of this takes place in interactions and through mediation where the mediators are usually bilingual. Mediators may be peers or adults.

(Gregory *et al.* 2004: 5)

We know that children learn to decode and interpret the particular graphic sign systems used by the culture(s) in which they live. We know too that these signs are socially constructed and that children make meaning from these through their interactions. Recent research looks at how, when children are able to play the role of 'teacher', they begin to re-interpret their own understanding in order to explain it to their peers.

Kenner (2004a) looked at what some six-year-old bilingual children were doing at a Community Saturday School where they were learning to write in their family language whilst learning literacy in English at their primary school. Peer teaching sessions were set up so that the children could teach one another how to write in Chinese or in Arabic or in Spanish – three languages with very different graphic systems. Here is an extract from what happened when Tala tried to teach Emily to write a word in Arabic – a language with which Emily was not familiar. Tala wanted to teach Emily to write her brother's name, Khalid. This is written in two parts, one for each syllable, because, according to the rules of Arabic writing, the letters 'alif' (which represent the 'a' sound) cannot join to any following letter. Tala wrote the word herself, in front of Emily, telling her what she was doing.

> Do that – it's like a triangle, but it's got a line like here ... go 'wheee' like this (as she finished with an upward stroke). Emily tried to follow this lead, saying as she wrote 'It looks like an "L" ... it looks like steps.' As Amina had done with Chinese, Emily was interpreting an unfamiliar script from the basis of English and of visual images. However, Tala realised that Emily had over-interpreted her instructions, with the result being too stylised and she commented 'It's not exactly like that – she's done steps'. Indeed, Emily's version looked like steps in a staircase rather than the fluid curves typical of Arabic writing. This difficulty continued during the lesson and to help her friend produce more appropriate writing, Tala resorted to a technique used by her own Arabic teacher. She provided a 'join-the-dots' version of the words required.
>
> (Kenner 2004a: 113)

You will see how in this small exchange the children demonstrate both a desire to learn from and teach one another: to share their skills as experts about their own languages and cultures, and to learn from their peers. This desire to share meaning across languages and literacies has been well documented by Datta (2000) and by D'Arcy (2002).

Learning styles and culture

In an earlier chapter we looked closely at play as a learning style and recognised its importance, but realised, too, that it is not the only way in which children and others learn. Romero (2004) looked at the different styles of learning she observed amongst the Pueblo children of New Mexico. In North America and in the United Kingdom and through much of Europe there is a strong emphasis on school readiness with parents being encouraged to 'educate' their children in the skills and knowledge which will allow them to succeed in school. In this way parents are being urged to build their children's cultural capital. In other countries preparation for success at school is less important than preparation for living in their community. In such communities there are things that children need to learn and these are, of course, related to the cultural beliefs and principles and values, which are linked to the economic survival of the group. Romero's writing is full of fascinating details about the lives of Pueblo children which we do not have time to explore here. We are going to examine some of the ways in which children are expected to learn.

In New Mexico the Pueblo children interact with primary caregivers on a daily basis and with secondary caregivers (those within the community) less regularly. Through all these interactions Pueblo children make and share meanings.

- *Learning by doing.* A key factor in the socialisation of Pueblo children is to allow the children to learn by doing. An example might be learning to bake pueblo bread in the large outdoor ovens where women work together and children are close at hand first watching and then doing. This is analogous with what Rogoff called guided participation
- *Silent learning.* Silent learning is sometimes called legitimate peripheral participation (Lave and Wenger 1991) and is where the child is on the periphery of some activity, silently observing and joining in at some level. The example cited by Romero is of a young child going with his father to the house where the older men smoke, drum and sing. The child intently watched what was happening and then silently imitated the behaviours he observed – including smoking his crayons! In an inner-London infant school a young boy with Down's syndrome in a mainstream class sat in and listened to the other children attempting to read, and watched intently what they did. After some months he was able to hold a book and to mimic the reading behaviours he had observed.
- *Role modelling.* As in all cultures children spend time watching their family and community members in interactions in the home and beyond. As they do this children begin to understand what behaviours, intonation, patterns and gestures define which roles. We have had examples of behaviours like this throughout this book, including the one of Luigi at the start of this chapter. For the Pueblo children there is some evidence that the roles they observe are the roles they aspire to – for example to be a traditional leader.
- *Mentoring.* Very close to all of the above, mentoring implies that the child will learn from an expert other – perhaps an older sibling or a parent or grandparent or a community member. The example cited by Romero is that of pottery making. At home the children observe the women potters and are exposed to the whole process. They may then go into the mountains with the potter to collect clay and other materials. They may be given pieces of clay to play with. Simple instructions may be given. Mainly, however, the child is an onlooker and is not expected to be a potter until adolescence and then specific teaching will be offered.

The family: transmission of beliefs and values

In coming to understand development as a cultural process, theorists have come up with the idea of the *developmental niche*. This is defined as being made up of three elements within the environments of the children that influence their development. Lansdowne (2005) refers to these as follows:

1   *The physical and social settings of the child.* This refers primarily to the child's family with its social patterns and the ways in which daily life is organised.
2   *The culturally regulated customs and practices.* This relates to how children are reared, what the relationship between care and education is and what the attitudes to such things as play or discipline or training are.
3   *The beliefs or ethno-theories of the parents.* This refers to the goals and priorities of the parents for their children and their views on how their children can best be 'prepared' to achieve these goals.

We have already noted that children do not live monocultural lives and that they are active players in making and transforming culture. But some indications of the circumstances which impact daily on the lives of children – particularly within the family – are helpful in building an understanding of development.

In some cultures the passing on of values and beliefs is seen as a way of handing a legacy to the children. In this sense it is helping children make meaning about life and death; or about creating a set of perspectives in order to organise their relationships with one another. So the passing on of values and beliefs involves making meaning of obligations, responsibility and rights (as well as roles). Children, through the exploration of these concepts, find their place in the world and explore belonging. In South Africa much emphasis is laid on the role of the family in transmitting cultural values and norms. This family socialisation is seen as one way of protecting children and preparing them for life within that society. In poor families it may happen that the older family members, aware of the poverty that exists, prepare their children for self-denial and self-regulation. An example is cited in Barbarin and Richter (2001) where the family deny the child sugar in order to prepare her for future life so that she will be prepared to accept food without sugar as a guest. Implicit in African culture is the obligation to cater for the needs of guests.

In South Africa, as in many cultures, one of the tasks of the family is to pass on religious cultural norms and practices. One of these is respect of ancestors. This involves a series of rights and rituals to mark rites of passage, to protect people from illness and from harm from the supernatural world. In Mexico the Day of the Dead is one of the most important cultural rituals. The Mexican attitude to death has sometimes been described as national fatalism. Death is feared but also made absurd through the images produced. Made of papier mâché or tin or fabric, skeletons and skulls are depicted riding horses, smoking cigars, dancing in the streets, wearing top hats. You can see clearly here how cultural tools are used to depict society, to comment on aspects of society and sometimes to transform society.

You will realise that there are many factors that impinge on how effectively families are able to nurture and socialise children. Included in these are family structure, family income, family health, family mobility and so on. In Southern Africa the ability of the family to nurture children and socialise them into the culture is being deeply damaged by the HIV/Aids pandemic. The disease has killed 4. 3 million and in the worse affected countries of Southern Africa something like 20 per cent of households are child-headed. Other children are being reared by grandparents. You can see from this how poverty itself can impinge on culture.

High culture: popular culture?

In the first chapter of this book we looked at how images of children have changed over time and looked at the paintings of Paula Rego, the Portuguese-born artist. We examined there how her own experiences of Portuguese imperialism affected her paintings, which are like visual fables and are drawn from a range of sources: the surreal paintings of Luis Bunuel and the early work of Walt Disney whom she described as 'a genius'. Rego's paintings could not be described as 'popular culture' yet Disney's work certainly falls into this category. So in her work she clearly draws on a range of influences including those from popular culture. You will remember that for Vygotsky, learning is to do with the transmission of culture: the passing on of the things pooled and discovered, adapted and changed, from generation to generation. This is not a passive but an essentially creative process. So Paula Rego created something new out of her experiences, observations, feelings and exposure to artefacts and other things. The Mexican artist Frida Kahlo was someone else who melded popular culture into her art. In an attempt to recognise and celebrate the indigenous culture of Mexico as opposed to the imposed Spanish imperial culture, she included the colours, the symbols, the patterns and the materials of this culture into her paintings. Cultures are not fixed, but change and develop. The art produced by Frida Kahlo, drawn from her unique experiences and the meanings she made from this, will be reflected in the work of others to come. Cultures change as innovations are made.

Both Bakhtin (1981) and Vygotsky (1978) saw that children's consciousness – their awareness of their world and those in it – exists only as part of the social and cultural worlds. It is others who induct children into signs and symbols that are used by both children and adults to interact with and enquire about the world. As children and adults continue to explore this, with the gaps between their understandings growing smaller as meanings are negotiated, children become more and more members of a community of sign-users. In other words it is through interactions with others in meaningful and relevant contexts that children become part of the world of reading, writing, mathematics, art, music and other symbolic systems. Vygotsky reminds us that children 'grow into the intellectual life of those around them' (1978: 88). Volosinov (1973) adds to this a reminder that even those sharing words or language are divided by things like class, religion, race, ethnicity and gender.

Stuart Hall and others in the Birmingham Centre for Cultural Studies in the 1960s and 1970s talked of *cultural relativity* looking at the web of strands that link state, society and cultural forms. This model of cultural relativity illustrates powerfully just how multilayered and multifaceted culture is; how it is made up of a myriad of discourses and is subject to change as individuals appropriate aspects of it.

In our culture there is a divide between what is called popular culture (the culture of the streets, the day-to-day lives of people) and what is known as high culture. High culture is often used to describe things like literature or art or opera or classical music. In effect, however, what is now known as high culture has been elevated to this 'higher' status having started off as things for the people in their everyday lives. One example is the opera *The Magic Flute,* originally written by Mozart as a popular opera and because he needed the money it would earn him. Partly what accounts for the changing view of what is popular culture is the relationship between popular culture and power in society. By power we mean things like control of the media, of education, of economic production.

Gramsci was an influential Marxist philosopher who looked at how the dominant classes manage to retain their control over those 'beneath' them in the social structures. He talked of *hegemony,* which he described as the process by which such powerful groups impose their power on others and maintain their hold once it has been established. Central to how the powerful class exercises power is not coercion or brute force, but a more subtle way of imposing a set of ideas, values, principles, beliefs, objectives, and cultural and political meanings. In other words, the people need to be persuaded of certain things in order to support them and the persuasion comes partially through popular culture. Think about the American electoral process and how much importance is attached to celebrity support, images, dress, the adoption of key songs and so on.

If you think about it you will realise that popular culture can equally act in the opposite direction. It can become the medium for helping those subject to powerful forces from above to resist. A famous case in point is what happened in Chile in South America where a strong and popular music developed from folk songs and where the singers were strongly opposed to the forces being massed against the people. The songs they wrote and sang became popular and powerful forces against the government – so powerful, in fact, that some of the singers, such as Victor Jara, were jailed and subsequently killed. In South Africa, too, music became an extremely powerful influence in the fight against apartheid.

The popular culture of children today is made up of a huge number of strands. Cartoon films offer images of violence but also of fantasy and gentleness and humour. Some children will watch Asian films. Some will listen and dance to popular music. Some will spend time dressing their dolls in doll-sized versions of adult clothes. Alongside that is the culture of the Harry Potter books and the Philip Pullman books and a proliferation of films and DVDs made, exclusively, for consumption by children. It is a long way from the childhood of the Middle Ages discussed in the first chapter. As societies have changed and cultures become globalised and increasingly commercialised, a whole children's culture has developed. Lash and Urry (1994) talk of the dematerialisation of products. By this they mean the impact of mass media (like television, the cinema and, of course, the internet) on products. These are dematerialised because of the speed with which such images are able to be conveyed across the globe. The effects of this may be regarded as paradoxical because they have the potential to bring about global homogenisation (as in the dominance of English as a language, and of American images of heroes and villains and so on) but also global differences. The creation of images of difference may be regarded as one of the outcomes of what is often described as the relativism that global culture brings.

One of the impacts of this globalisation is to make more difficult the concept of society. Societies are less and less able to secure their cultural and defining boundaries. In Tuscany, for example, local people fear that the influx of English home-owners is diluting their culture and their traditions and resent the fact that children want to learn English because of all that is available to them through the internet, the cinema and videos.

We talked earlier about how a culture for children has developed over the past several decades. Even this is becoming more and more homogenised as the range of goods available becomes more freely available throughout the world – where people can afford these goods. However, Prout (2005) reminds us that within any one particular place childhood experience is also becoming more diverse because the range of products is greater and hence children can select to operate within different niches and construct different identities.

Becoming integrated into a cultural group or niche involves understanding the rituals and rules and the language of that group and of being able to participate in those rules and rituals. Becoming a member of a group, then, means that the rules have to be inferred. Just as children new to any setting, for example a classroom, have to learn the language and rules of that setting in order to develop the new identity of 'member' or 'friend' or 'pupil', so they have to develop what we might call a repertoire of cultural registers in order to be admitted. Inevitably there are groups with a perceived higher status than others, and, just as in the adult world of work and institutions, aspects of 'gatekeeping' operate. Sarangi and Roberts argue that 'learning "how to be" and "how to act" involve developing an understanding of events, feelings, roles and statuses ... as relative newcomers participate in new social practices' (2002: 200).

Although Sarangi and Roberts are looking at adult newcomers to professional institutions (medicine) their analysis can equally well apply to children. At the age of eight Hannah wanted to be part of a particular group of girls who were perceived by her to be 'high status'. In order to do this she analysed what shared cultural capital they had and then set about working on her own cultural capital so that she would be able to use the languages (in the broadest sense) they used, to allow her access to the group. The girls whose group she aspired to join were interested in pop music and dance. The children already in the group are the 'gatekeepers' – the ones who decide who to admit and who to exclude. Hannah engaged in the intricate cognitive task of working out how to align her actions to those of the group. She has not, of course, had to sit down and read the works of Bourdieu to do this. She has had to work out for herself what would allow her access to the chosen group. In other words she has made herself develop cultural competence in an aspect of popular culture. She has also had to deal with the uncomfortable realisation that one of her closest friends, a child fairly new to the class and a speaker of English as another language, was often not able to align herself to the group. Erikson and Schultz (1982) talk of gatekeeping encounters as being neither neutral nor objective but suggest that they are like a carefully rigged game in favour of those who are most like the members of the group in terms of both social background and communication styles.

In terms of alignment the children in Hannah's group of choice are all girls. It is unclear whether or not boys are excluded because they are not aligned or because they choose not to engage in what is described by the girls themselves as 'a girl thing'. Vivian Gussin Paley's work (1984) has been influential in describing how both boys and girls use the opportunity to create stories from their own experience and 'act' out their feelings and concerns within the classroom. Many of her vivid accounts show how boys, using superhero play, may cloak their feelings of sorrow or anxiety in becoming more powerful than ever. According to Paley, girls, by contrast, appear to have a need to explore emotions and relationships, but often within the relatively safe context of fairy tales. Girls nowadays have access to a wide range of stories exploring issues of relationships and emotions and it seems that in many playgrounds these are the stories currently being played out (Smidt 2004).

Building on culture in play: symbol weaving

In looking at how children draw on culture – including popular culture – in their play, it is soon evident that children draw on different texts and influences, weaving them together into a new theme. Indeed Dyson (1993) describes this process *as symbol weaving* where the children draw on myriad cultural influences and references as they play or write or draw or model. She reminds us that it is as children that we utilise all the materials we encounter in our lives to use in expressing our thoughts and ideas – unaware, as yet, of the barriers society erects between good and bad, high culture and popular culture. Kress (2000) uses the term *communicational webs* to describe children's ability to draw on a huge range and variety of texts and artefacts in their own attempts at storying and meaning making.

As children move from one cultural space to another they are engaged in what is sometimes called *border crossing*. Many examples of border or boundary crossing were observed by Pahl (1999) in the nursery she visited in order to do her research. Those engaged or working with children may need to be able to identify and understand the sources children draw on. As children are exposed to more and more influences on television, DVDs, the internet and other media, it becomes more and more difficult for adults to recognise what Geertz (1983) calls their 'local knowledge'. This refers to the detailed knowledge children carry within them of their home, community and local details and the detailed personal knowledge they have of worlds in their heads. The old adage of knowing what children know and understanding its relevance remains crucial. It is only by doing this that we are able to have a fair image of the child of the twenty-first century.

Summing up

In this chapter we have moved on to looking at the child in culture and seeing how the child works both to use the cultural tools available to him or her and to construct meaning. We have looked at how culture is not one fixed thing, but something dynamic, and at how children do not live in one culture only, but inhabit the cultures that apply to them in a range of intersecting discourses, one of which involves what is known as 'popular culture'. We have looked at what the children 'acquire' in their interactions with others of their culture and at how this may help or hinder them in other cultures. We have touched on the work of Bronfennbrenner, Bourdieu and Gramsci, learned more about Vygotsky and been introduced to some of the current work on multilingualism being done by Kenner and Gregory. So our twenty-first-century child is now seen as able to operate differently in different contexts, using what is relevant from her culture to apply to another, and able to share aspects of one culture with others.

Questions

- What have you understood about the role of culture and of how individuals and groups are represented within cultures on children's construction of their identity?
- Do you believe that cultural capital is inevitably linked to success or failure?
- What does a syncretic analysis allow us to do in terms of explaining how children operate differently in different contexts?

Chapter 7

The child as role maker

In this chapter we start to think about how children position themselves in different contexts and play the roles assigned to them within these contexts. As a preparation for this we will look at children engaged in 'role-playing'. This involves looking at how children construct their identity, which is complex, and at what factors impinge on this. So we look at examples such as what it means to be the youngest or the oldest in the family; we look at the child as a single child or as the member of an extended family; and we examine the issues involved in being a boy or a girl. We look at the child as friend, as pupil, as worker, as member of various groups and so on. And we draw on the words of authors and thinkers who may not be experts in child development but show us aspects of the roles we play in our lives.

> At first I'd done my very best to fit in and be good. We had been set a project just before we started last autumn, we all had to write an essay called 'What I Did in my Summer Holidays'. I was anxious to do it well because I knew they thought I couldn't read or anything, not having been to school early enough. I did it slowly in my best handwriting, proud that some of the others could only print. We read them out one by one, then gave them to the teachers. It was all the same, fishing, swimming, picnics, Walt Disney. 32 essays about gardens and frog spawn. I was at the end of the alphabet, and I could hardly wait. The teacher was the kind of woman who wanted her class to be happy. She called us lambs, and had told me in particularly not to worry if I found anything difficult.
> 'You'll soon fit in' she soothed.
> I wanted to please her, and trembling with anticipation. I started my essay ... 'This holiday I went to Colwyn Bay with our church camp.'
> The teacher nodded and smiled.
> 'It was very hot, and Auntie Betty, whose leg was loose anyway, got sunstroke and we thought she might die.'
> The teacher began to look a bit worried, but the class perked up.
> 'But she got better, thanks to my mother who stayed up all night struggling mightily.'
> 'Is your mother a nurse?' asked the teacher, with quiet sympathy.
> 'No, she just heals the sick.'
> ...
> When we came back from Colwyn Bay Next Door had had another baby but there are so many of them Next Door we don't know whose it is. My mother gave them some potatoes from the yard but they said they weren't a charity and threw them back over the wall.

In Jeanette Winterson's novel *Oranges Are Not the Only Fruit* Jeanette lived at home with her mother and father. She was an only child in a strange family dominated by God and the church and with clear-cut divides between enemies and friends. She knew she was special and was curious about school but her mother refused to send her until she was instructed to do so. She did not know what to expect: her mother referred to school, negatively, as a Breeding Ground. You can see from this extract how little opportunity this single child has had to develop the language and the gestures and the positions she needed in order to become a school pupil. Her cultural capital clearly did not equip her to adapt easily to school and playing the role of school pupil remained difficult. Her home experiences were so diverse from those of her schoolmates and so remote from what the school expected and she was so immersed in the language of her home and church that she was, at first, unable to make the moves necessary to allow her admission to this role.

Constructing identity: playing roles

When you consider who you are you will almost certainly be sure of your name and your age and your address and your position in the family. You may be sure of what it is you do and what things you enjoy. But when it comes to defining who you are in terms of your identity you will find this much more difficult to state. Women may define themselves as 'someone's mum' or 'someone's wife' or 'someone's daughter.' But identities, like culture, are not simple or single, but complex and dynamic. Over the course of our lives, we come to define who we are according to where we are, who we are with, what we are doing and how we are observed. Here is what a very old woman said when looking over the course of her life:

> When I was a child we lived in a lovely house near the sea. I was the oldest and the apple of my father's eye. Anything I wanted was mine. I didn't go to school but had a governess and we read romantic novels and listened to music and collected shells. I was pretty and privileged. Then my family had to emigrate. We were Jews living in Greece and life was becoming intolerable so we set off for South Africa where we had some distant relatives. Soon after arriving I went to the University. And there I found a different me. I was a good student – enjoyed studying and enjoying being different. Because I had come from Europe and spoke Greek I was admired. I was also pretty and that helped.
>
> After I graduated I married and had a child. Two more roles to add to my growing repertoire. But these were not roles that I excelled at. I didn't like the restrictions I felt were imposed on me by being someone's wife and I found motherhood deeply unsatisfying. I loved my child dearly but the thought of spending day after day with him drove me to despair.
>
> I decided to go out to work and employ another woman to look after my child. I managed to find work in a law office where I met interesting people and was thought to be efficient and organised. I enjoyed being in control. I played the role of manager well and enjoyed the recognition I got from colleagues and peers.
>
> (Personal communication, 2005)

You can see how this woman played a range of roles as time and place and circumstance changed. You can see, too, how her sense of her own identity altered according to her perceptions of how she viewed herself and believed that others viewed her.

The human infant begins to define his or her identity first by starting to see him- or herself both as unique but also as connected to others. For most infants these others are members of the immediate family and perhaps the more extended family and then, perhaps, the local community and neighbourhood. Here the child begins to interact with people and in doing this learns to see others as having feelings and having intentions. Young children begin to pay attention to what others say and do: in part they mimic what they see and hear and they also internalise ways of acting, ways of speaking and ways of being. These build into a store of memories which can be drawn on in the complex scripts they will develop to play out the roles they need to play.

So the young child who starts to play at being different people is, in effect, trying out what it feels like to be in someone else's shoes.

> Lilliane is playing in the garden with her younger brother Thomas. She is being the mother and he is the baby. She holds his hand very tightly in hers and tells him to walk more quickly. 'Come on!' she says, in a loud and irritable voice. 'I am sick of telling you. Come on! We are going to be late.' And she pulls his arm to hurry him along.
>
> (Personal observation)

A very simple role-play script, but what a lot is revealed. Here the child tries out what it feels like to be an adult – a mother, whose child is not walking fast enough. She is able to select the tone of voice and the speech patterns she must have heard adults (her mother and others) use when angry.

> Zwelethini is the older child. Busi is her younger brother. The children live with their mother and life is hard, particularly for Zwelethini who must look after Busi, help her mother in the house, go to school and, in the afternoons, help out in the village. Zwelethini loves Busi but is envious of his status as both boy and younger child. Notice how this emerges in their play.
>
> Zwelethini: Now I am going to be the baby and you are my big brother and you have to look after me.
>
> Busi: Don't want to.
>
> Zwelethini: If you want me to play with you, you must do it. I am the baby and I am crying and you must bring me some food to eat.
>
> Busi scrabbles in a box and brings her a handful of leaves.
>
> Zwelethini: You must mash this for me and feed me. I love being the baby. I don't have to do anything and you have to do all the work.
>
> Busi: I want to be the baby now.

You will remember that often the first role play children engage in is playing out their domestic roles and when they start moving beyond the immediate family they move on to playing more functional roles. Here is an example of three children playing school, taken from Ann William's piece called 'Playing School in Multiethnic London'. Wahida is ten and Sayeda is eight years old.

> Wahida: Now we are going to do homophones. Who knows what a homophone is? No one? OK. I'll tell you one and then you're going to do some by yourselves. Like watch. One watch is your time watch, like 'What's the time' watch: and another

watch is 'I'm watching you. I can see you ...'So Sayeda, you wrote some in your books haven't you? Can you please tell me some, please. Can you only give me three, please.

Sayeda: Oh. I wanted to give you five.

Wahida: No, Sayeda, we haven't got enough time. We've only got five minutes to assembly.

Sayeda: Son is the opposite of daughter ... And sun is ... It shines on the sky so bright ....

(Williams 2004: 63)

In this wonderful example you see Wahida using the language of the classroom and the intonation patterns used by teachers. She is clearly in control and inducts her younger sister not only into the mysteries of homophones but into the practices and the language of school. Later, in the same chapter, Williams cites a pretend telephone conversation between-eleven-year old Lee and seven-year-old Cathy.

Lee (pretending to phone):   Hello Miss Rhodes?

Cathy (talking with an upper-class accent):   Yees

Lee: Your daughter's gone on a trip and she won't be back until about six o'clock tomorrow night.

Cathy: Has she now! Not again!!

Lee: I imagine she stayed overnight at school so I'm very sorry about that.

Cathy: She said she was writing a story.

(Williams 2004: 60)

The children are consummate players of this game They are able to mimic the language patterns of people in authority and to introduce into their role play explorations about some of the issues that currently concern them – in this case possibly excuses, lies and explanations.

In their role play children sometimes use the objects themselves to play the roles they have chosen for them. In this sense the objects become the living beings – puppets in the hands of their puppet-masters, the children. In doing this the children then adopt the voices and the language they have agreed on in designing and enacting their negotiated chosen scenario. Here are Hannah, aged nine, and Ben, aged seven, playing a complex game that went on over days. This is a very brief extract:

Ben (in a high-pitched voice, manipulating a Lego Knight he has made in one hand): You will do exactly as I do – exactly! If you do not do this you will die spectacularly.

Han (also in a high pitched voice, wielding a Groovy Girl doll): Sir, sir, I beg you. Be kind to me. We were only practising our spells. We did not intend any harm. (Note the use of the language of books.)

Ben (high-pitched voice again): Practising? Well you weren't very good at it, were you. They would not want you in Hogwarts. (Note the reference to the fictional world of Harry Potter)

Han (out of role – using her normal voice): Shall I get one of those (points to a Lego Bionicle) to be the chief?

Ben (in role, nods): Now, do as I say or you will ...

Hannah (in role): ... pay the price.

Ben (out of role): How much is the price?

Hannah (out of role): Not money, silly. It means you will have to pay for what you have done – get punished. We need to decide on a good punishment.
Ben (out of role): I know. A good one. We could make them play a game of chess and then they could be stalemated.
Hannah (out of role): Or checkmated. Which is which? I never remember.
Ben (in role): I challenge you to a chess match. And if you don't win and I don't win we will be stalemated. And if we are stalemated then I will not play with you any more. You won't be my best friend any more.

In this extract you see more of the children trying out voices, going in and out of role, than you see of them constructing identity. But you can see how they draw on strands from their normal lives, from their toys, from the books they read and the films they see and the games they play, to sort out some issues. Later in the play the toys get involved in a complex sequence relating to issues of friendship and power – issues that deeply concern these children. The identities they play include being a victim in the sense of exploring what it feels like when a friend chooses not to play with you, or chooses someone instead of you, or makes you feel inadequate and unloved. These are important issues in the lives of young children, trying to sort out who they are in relation to important others – in other words, trying to sort out their identity.

In all these examples of role play we see children involved in answering the questions they have set themselves and all of these questions appear to be of the 'What if?' variety. What if my friend is nasty to me? What if I could be the younger child? What if I was really angry? Engaging in the play they must make decisions about who is involved in the play, what is involved in the play, where the action takes place and what the central theme is. This requires them to develop and use a range of complex cognitive and social skills including skilful negotiation; logical sequencing of events; drawing on and combining their experiences; symbolisation; and speaking and listening. As they move into more abstract play the same principles apply. The children can create their own script, negotiate about who will play what part and use 'what is to hand' to represent anything they agree.

The social construction of gender

Mindy Blaise (2005) is an early childhood teacher and one who has moved away from the traditional influence of child development, largely because her interest in gender has led her to believe that she needs to take a more justice-based political stance, examining what it means for children to be, for example, girls, or to be Asian Americans or British children of mixed race. She contends that developmentally appropriate practice (DAP), with its model of the naturally developing child, conceals the ways in which gender influences a child's experiences and how the child interprets these experiences, and also fails to address the different ways in which children's gender itself, together with their experiences of gender, affect the child's learning and development. She adopts what she calls a feminist poststructuralist approach which is an approach that looks at issues of power in society. Poststructuralism becomes feminist, she argues, when matters of gender become a central concern. She draws heavily on the work of Foucault (1979) who believed that power operates in all relationships and is expressed through discourse. Any consideration of how children construct gender would need to take account of power and this would be true for constructing race or class or disability.

Alternatively one could adopt a sociocultural approach to considering how children construct the image of boy or girl. The approach of the socioculturalists to gender is that it is a product neither of biology nor simply of socialisation. Rather it is a product of human meaning-making. So the concept of gender which we construct makes the maleness or femaleness of people significant. A famous piece of research cited in Lloyd and Duveen (1990) makes this clear. Boy babies were dressed in pink and girl babies in blue. Blue and pink are, as you may know, the colours often used to define gender in the US and Europe. People meeting the babies for the first time assumed those in blue were boys and those in pink were girls and treated them accordingly. So the girls were called 'pretty' and were cuddled and treated gently when they hurt themselves. Boys, on the other hand, were called 'big' and 'strong' and played with in a more boisterous way. The meaning of this is that the socially constructed markers of gender (the colours) affected the ways in which the children were treated. And it does not require a huge step of logic to recognise that the way in which children are treated will affect their images of themselves. Gender, in this sense, operates in all cultures and powerfully affects the images children create of their own gender identity.

In this sense gender becomes something that we 'do'. It runs so deeply through our society that we assume that it is genetic. But socioculturalists hold firm to their belief that gender, like culture, is a human construct. Look at the gender symbols built into this portrait:

> In Covent Garden in London a man was pushing his small child in a stroller. He was clearly enjoying the experience and chatting away to the child, and appreciating the smiles given to both of them by passers-by. These passers-by were 'doing gender' in the sense that they clearly liked the sight of this father caring so lovingly for his child and they gave him signs of approbation. Moreover the child was dressed in blue dungarees and had long curls. It was impossible to tell from the clothing what the sex of the child was. But when the father handed his child a doll the child's gender was being 'done'. Those who saw the child with the doll would respond to the child as a 'girl'.
>
> (Personal observation, 2006)

What happens when children construct their gender identity? Do they simply learn to adopt the roles that are assigned to them by society? If this was the case there would be no change and one role would be passed on from generation to generation. But we know that this is not the case. Francis (1998) believed that identity is not fixed but fluid and that it is positioned by the different discourses (or contexts and interactions) that individuals engage in. This discursive positioning is something we have touched on earlier in this book when we looked at the views of children and childhood and how these changed over time and place.

Walkerdine (1988) was interested in the reasons for the observed failure of girls to do well at mathematics at school in the 1970s. She found that the dominant discourse about girls and schooling operating at the time was that girls were doing mathematics 'the wrong way'. This discourse drew on the views of Piaget with their emphasis on the child as logical and rational problem-solver. Girls, in solving mathematics problems, tended to be more systematic and disciplined. But since these skills were not, at that time, seen as being 'useful' for mathematics, the girls were defined and positioned by their teachers and their schools and, subsequently, by themselves. How many women do you know who regard themselves as being weak at mathematics or physics?

As we have seen, the dominant discourse in the 1970s was that girls will struggle to succeed at mathematics or at physics. It is fortunate that no one is powerless to resist the impact of the dominant discourse on their construction of identity. Resistance is the term used to describe how those who may be thought of as powerless can actually exercise power in order to resist what is being said and thought of them. In other words, human beings are not merely the victims of their positioning, but can actively challenge this in order to change both themselves and the dominant discourse. You will realise that power is a key factor in determining discourse positions. Here is an example to illustrate this:

> Shameem fell in love with an English boy and wanted to go and live with him. Her parents were outraged. It was customary in their culture for girls to be entered into arranged marriages and the thought of their beloved daughter living with someone outside of marriage was bad enough: the thought of her living with an English boy was impossible. Shameem is almost powerless in this situation. Her parents hold the power in determining her future. She is almost powerless, but can, of course, decide to challenge the dominant discourse by moving out to live with her chosen boyfriend, although the social consequences might well be very painful for her.

The role of *power* in discourse is complex and operates like a web or a network, according to Foucault (1979). It is like a web or network in the sense that those involved in a discourse can both exercise power and be affected by others exercising power. It permeates all relationships from the most intimate and personal to the institutional. Jacques Derrida (1972), the French philosopher, was responsible for introducing the concept of *deconstruction,* which involves examining the ways in which something – such as gender, for example – has been socially constructed and looking at what the consequences are. The word 'deconstruction' might make you think that Derrida is talking about destroying something; on the contrary it is a very careful way of unpicking or unfolding to see what has been hidden or avoided or left out, or of considering what different routes might have been taken, or of examining the use of taken-for-granted concepts. Deconstruction is a really useful tool for examining something carefully.

Children actively construct identities through 'reading' and interpreting what they encounter. But in coming to make meaning, not any interpretation is open to the child. Children may construct many meanings but some are going to be limited according to the prevailing norms and principles, or by the values and the customs of the community or culture or society in which identity construction is taking place.

> Johan is four years old. He lives in Bradford. He loves nothing more than to dress up in the clothes in the dressing up box in his nursery. And most of all he likes to dress up in a particular pink dress and drape a purple scarf over his shoulders and totter around in shoes that are too big for him. But he will not do this after lunch and when asked why he explained that he didn't want his mum to see him dressed like that because 'it's girly and I'm not a pouf'. He fears his mum will tell his dad.

Let us now try to deconstruct this small case study. This child appears to want to explore what it might feel like to be a girl and he does this by dressing in girls' clothes. It is clear that this is something that is acceptable in the nursery. But Johan has internalised something about the powerful discourse operating in his family and fears the disapproval of his father. The use of homophobic language gives an insight into the language accepted at home including the negative implications that some of it carries.

There is evidence that, from the earliest years, children demonstrate strong opinions about their gender positioning. The social construction of gender operates in various ways. Children encounter views on gender at home (as in the case of Johan above), and in their community, hearing about what things are appropriate for boys and what for girls. Sex-role stereotyping becomes cemented by practices in society which harden the gender roles. But since we are suggesting that there is no one fixed self or identity and that identity is constructed and not imposed, children are able to fluctuate in their identity. There are, however, some situations in which children's freedom to construct their identity is limited by race or class or language or physical ability.

Gender continues to be an extremely significant factor in the childhood of millions of children throughout the world. Over generations there have been huge discrepancies in the numbers of boys and girls being born, surviving and dying in different groups at different times. In Africa and Europe and South America there are currently slightly more boys born than girls. This appears to have a biological base because boys have a slightly higher death rate in infancy. But in China and in India and some other countries there are many more boys born than girls. The reasons for this are, like everything, complex and involve the fact that in some countries boys are more valued than girls, partly because they will provide the family with an heir. Where boys are more highly prized in a society the consequences for girls can be death, as is sometimes suggested in the one-child-per-family policy in China.

Opportunities available to boys and girls will vary according to economics, to philosophy, to values and to place. In many countries throughout the world girls still have fewer educational opportunities than boys. The reason for this might be the traditional expectation in many societies that the roles of girls are to be mothers and wives. And in these cultures early marriages sometimes put an end to schooling. The consequence is that literacy levels of women are often significantly lower than those of men and this has an impact on the women themselves and on their children. There is evidence that shows that educated girls are less likely to die in childbirth and give birth to fewer children. The children themselves are less likely to die in infancy, are better nourished and suffer less from illnesses (UNICEF 2000).

Language, identity and roles

We have touched on this in Chapter 6 when we looked at the story of Antti Jalava and his experiences of having to go to school where the language of his home was neither used nor recognised. There is a considerable body of research documenting how closely language is tied to identity. People who have been uprooted and moved to a country which uses another language, or people living in countries where their own language is marginalised and not given recognition, suffer loss of identity and some theorists describe this process in very emotive terms by talking of the genocide of minority languages.

Some twenty years ago two children, born in Britain, to parents from mainland Turkey who had neglected to renew their permission to stay in Britain, were deported. The older child,

> Zeynep, was eight years old when they left. English was her first language – her mother tongue – and she was the spokesperson for her entire family, talking to reporters and officials and others. When they got to Istanbul she found herself in a country where she did not know the language and where she was teased for speaking English. She quickly learned to speak Turkish but, in the process, lost every word of her English. Now, twenty years later, her English is not that of a native speaker of the language and she is having to go to English language classes to try and regain it. She says 'When I couldn't communicate in English I felt like nobody. I didn't know who I was any more. And when I learned Turkish I didn't want to speak English in case I become different again. It was terrible.'

Zeynep, at the age of eight, had been a fluent and articulate speaker of English. One of the key roles in her childhood was to be the spokesperson for her family in many situations – at school, at the local clinic, in connection with officials and so on. When she had to go and live in another country where her language was mocked, she gave up her mother-tongue to protect herself and devoted her time to learning a new language – that of her new country. She did not just bury her first language but managed to lose it almost entirely. The links with her self-esteem and identity are clear.

In his first novel, Tash Aw, a young writer in London, writes a story set in what was then Malaya. In setting the scene for the dramatic events of the story he talks of the narrator's ancestors who came from the south of China – from Guangdong and Fujian provinces, where, he tells us, the people spoke two distinct languages. He says:

> This is important because your language determined your friends and enemies. People in our town speak mainly Hokkien, but there are number of Hakka speakers too ... The literal translation of 'Hakka' is 'guest-people', descendants of tribes defeated in ancient battles and forced to live outside city walls. These Hakkas are considered by the Hokkiens and other Chinese here to be really very low class, with distinct criminal tendencies. No doubt they were responsible for the historical tension and bad feelings with the Hokkiens in these parts. Their one advantage, often used by them in exercising subterfuge and cunning, is the similarity of their language to Mandarin, the noble and stately language of the Imperial Court, which makes it easy for them to disguise their dubious lineage. This is largely how Uncle Toby, who has become a hotel tycoon ('a *hotelier*' he says) managed to convince bank managers and the public at large that he is a man of education (Penang Free School and the London School of Economics) when really he is like my father – unschooled and really very uncultured. He has, to his credit, managed to overcome that most telltale sign of Hakka backwardness, which is the lack of the 'h' sound in their language and the resulting (and quite frankly, ridiculous) 'f' which comes out in its place whether speaking Mandarin, Malay or even English.
>
> (Aw 2005: 8)

This extract is full of snobbery and prejudice, but it highlights some salient features about how some socially aspiring people determinedly lose or change their language in order to be perceived differently. In this way they attempt to change their identity in order to play the particular roles in society they aspire to. If you consider this carefully you will realise that there are many people in your own society who try to change their language or dialect or accent in order to become more acceptable to others or more successful. Language is intimately connected to power.

Just how closely language is associated with identity, self-esteem and a sense of dignity is illustrated by Primo Levi in his book *The Drowned and the Saved*. As you may know, Levi was a survivor of Auschwitz, living for long enough to write poignant, powerful and bitter accounts of what he experienced and witnessed in the camp. Living in the camp were those whose first languages were Yiddish, Italian, Greek, Hungarian, French and German. The language of the camps became something else – something unique – tied to the camps, to the place and the time. It was described by a German Jewish philosopher, Klemperer, as the *Lingua Tertii Imperii* – the language of the Third Reich. Levi notes that where violence is inflicted on people, it is also inflicted on language. For the Italians, the attacks on the language spoken in particular regions of Italy and on some of the forms of language, described as either barbaric or servile, did much to damage the self-esteem of the inmates. In Auschwitz the word to eat was *fressen*, a word used almost exclusively for animals. In Ravensbruck, the only camp exclusively for women, two words were used to describe them: one was *Schmutzstuck*, which means dirty or garbage, and the other *Schmuckstuck*, which means jewel. You will have heard of the term 'Muselmann', which means Muslim, which was used to describe those worn-out ravaged prisoners close to death. The reasons for this are unclear although Levi suggests they could refer either to fatalism or to the head bandages which might have resembled a 'turban' (Levi, 1998: 77).

But Levi notes that possessing a language of potential use within the camps – i.e. German – was not a luxury but a life-saving necessity. He noted that those prisoners who did not understand German died within the first ten days after their arrival. The fact that they could not communicate meant that they could do nothing to ameliorate their conditions, even though they would almost certainly have perished in any case. This is complex stuff. The Nazi kommandants did not denigrate their own language, German – that civilised, sophisticated and respected language of Schiller and Goethe – but used a bastardised version and were thus able to retain an image of themselves as 'civilised'. In stark contrast the prisoners, deprived of their liberty, their families, their hair, their names and their language descended into an impossible anonymity.

In another of Levi's books, *The Truce*, which looks at what happened when the camps were liberated, he describes the tragic story of a three-year-old child named Hurbinek. He tells us: 'Hurbinek was a nobody, a child of death, a child of Auschwitz' (1979: 197). The child was alone, paralysed from the waist down, unable to speak at all. The name had been given to him and his eyes were full of anger and anguish. A fifteen-year-old boy in the camp tended to Hurbinek, brought him food to eat, cleaned him and talked to him slowly and carefully in Hungarian. After a week of doing this the older boy told the others that Hurbinek could say a word: what the word was no one knew, nor did they know what language it was in, but it was apparent the child was attempting to communicate. Levi tells us that the child experimented with making sounds – desperate to be understood – and even though there were speakers of all the languages of Europe, no one could understand him.

Hurbinek who was 3 years old and perhaps had been born in Auschwitz and had never seen a tree; Hurbinek, who had fought like a man, the last breath, to gain his entry into the world of men, from which a bestial power had excluded him Hurbinek; the nameless, whose tiny forearm – even his – bore the tattoo of Auschwitz; Hurbinek died in the first days of March 1945, free but not redeemed. Nothing remains of him: he bears witness through these words of mine.

(Ibid. 198)

As part of playing roles human beings make stories to allow them to explore the different roles that they – and others – play. Here they are free to explore every facet of their constructed identity and build inner and outer dialogues. You can find evidence of this in the autobiographies people write or the self-portraits they paint. You will remember that Bakhtin (1981) explored the ways in which we create images for others of others and of ourselves. He is considering the process of self-formation in both life and art. He suggests that there are three elements to doing this. There is firstly the construction of *how others appear* for the individual and this might include significant role models or influential people. Then there is the way in which the individual analyses *how he or she appears to others*, which might be called their social persona. And finally there is the question of *how the individual appears to the self* – in other words self-identity. Implicit in this is the mixture of the internal and the external. All of these notions are constructed initially inside families and hugely influenced by culture. Bakhtin believes that the story we create in words or symbols or pictures or role play is what gives coherence to the constant re-writing of self.

Stories from the streets of Lima: constructing peer identity

Where children are born determines to a large extent the roles they need to learn to play in life. Children born into middle-class families in Europe or the United Kingdom learn, first, to play the role of family member. Their position in the family (only child, oldest, youngest, etc. and gender) will affect the roles they play within the family and then beyond the family. But for millions of children in the world the demands of life are harsher and require that children have to play a series of roles related to the economical needs of the family.

In this section we will start by looking at the realities for a group of boys living in Lima in Peru and having to work in order to bring money into the family. The accounts are drawn from the work of Antonella Invernizzi (2003). For the purposes of examining how the children learn to position themselves we need a working definition of 'work'. Bolle de Ball (1987) defines work as a set of social links, understood as the concrete ties of an individual (e.g. the links between competitors or formed between collaborators) and the meaning attributed to these ties (which have a symbolic aspect which helps the child's construction of identity). The ties will be socioeconomic (i.e. the material benefits); sociocultural (i.e. the relationships with other workers and the way in which the child either belongs or does not) and socio-psychological (self-image and the ability to change the environment). In this sense work is defined as a social activity.

It will not surprise you to learn that the children we will be looking at come from the poorest groups in society. Working on the street is sometimes the only occupations open to these families and their children. These are also primarily urban children. The impossible demands of such urban lives is damaging traditional family roles with women having constantly to redefine their roles in order to adjust to the severe economic pressures.

Ten-year-old Marco began working on the streets when his parents separated. At first he sold cakes made by his mother and carried provisions to the market. Soon after, he went to live with his father, where he did not have to work but where he was neglected and frequently verbally abused. He went out onto the streets without his father's knowledge and enjoyed being able to explore the city and its people. There he met a

bookseller called Jorge who became a key figure in his socialisation. Marco began buying his own books and re-selling them. He learned techniques and the language of the
market – talking about the need to have capital and stock and the need to invest. Marco
tried contributing some of his earnings to the family's meagre capital, but his father
would not accept this and became angry. Marco felt that his father felt slighted and that
his attempt to help the family was seen as insulting. A real tension was building
between his father and his 'street father', Jorge. Marco's own analysis was that people on
the street respected what he did and treated him as an adult. He said that on the street
he came to know people, to accept them and to negotiate. He also encountered racial
discrimination.

In another case of a street worker a young child, earning money by shining shoes, was
involved not only in earning money but in managing a proportion of the money earned.
This is what he tells us his mother said: 'When you work ... don't give me (the money)!
When you go to school, don't ask me for things, buy them ... But money ... don't waste
it.' Sometimes the work children do is work as part of a family team where the children
play their roles as key workers. The lives of street children are characterised by different
phases as they become full workers. At first there is the introduction to street work, followed by working in order to survive. This is followed by work as a game, involving play
and peers. Then there is work as the search for identity, recognising skills and achieve-
ments, and finally there are the possibilities of getting out of street work. Let us look at
what happens to children who have passed through the subsistence phase and begin to be
able to see work as a game. At the centre of the lives of these children are their peers and
for the child good work is work that allows time to meet friends and talk to them.

Some of the girls working as sellers in Lima attempt to avoid having to sell in one
fixed place but seek to become itinerant sellers, allowing them time to explore things
like lifts and departments stores and to look at the goods on display in the shops which
would not be available in their poor neighbourhoods. Invernizzi tells us that the physical exploration of cities is an important feature of the life of child workers. Freedom to
roam is a matter of prestige for these children as they establish their work identities.
Later it will be the possession of either some training or a fixed sales pitch which will be
highly prized.

In the next stage of this process the child looks for status and positive social recognition. Work is at the heart of the child's identity and the skills the child has acquired
become important. What happens to children after this is uncertain. What is clear is
that many children seek to escape the street. Boys tend to move away from their
mother's pitch quite early on and when work becomes the thing that defines him, a boy
will look for some activity that will bring him status and social recognition. First then
the boy must become independent and free himself of his mother, and second, he seeks
work that might be defined as masculine as opposed to the more female-associated
activities of selling. Many boys seek to develop the skills required to work in a trade like
building or plumbing.

For girls the onset of adolescence is a turning point. Still being on the street carries a
social stigma but opportunities are few elsewhere. Some may find a job in a market stall
or as a domestic servant. But the research suggests that the majority of these girls
remain at fixed sites until adulthood. So on this tricky path children have to position
themselves differently at different stages, acquire different ways of behaving and speaking and playing a range of roles.

Glauser (1997) looked at street children in Asuncion and spent six years working with them and writing up his findings. He reminds us that street children are not a homogenous group and the term is used to talk about both children who work on the street and children who live on the street. He found that children who just work on the street use it differently from those who live on the street. For those living on the street this is home in the sense that it is here they need to build social relationships. But their lives living on the streets are unstable and subject to sudden and sometimes violent change. Glauser carefully considers the impact on children of losing their family ties (which often happens because of the difficulties of the lives of the children and of their family members) and he believes that this is something very damaging, particularly in developing countries where the family is so important and where society provides little safety net for those who lose the support of families.

Carraher *et al.* (1985) carried out a study to assess children's mathematical competence with a group of street children in Brazil (aged between nine and fifteen years). They all came from poor families and were involved in working on the streets rather than living on the streets. Most were in school and all were involved in aspects of buying or selling and handling money and financial transactions. An interesting aspect of the test given to the children was that it was given to them in two contrasting contexts. The first time children were asked questions about the actual transactions in which they were engaged and were asked to give verbal responses. The 'test' took place on the street or in the market. Next the children were given imaginary money problems to solve, and these were given in more formal settings. Not surprisingly the children achieved far higher scores when they were questioned about real events *in situ* than when questioned about imaginary events out of context.

Stories of child soldiers

You may think that the terrible phenomenon of child soldiers is something new or something limited to Africa. In effect there have been child soldiers since the Middle Ages when, in parts of Europe, young boys were apprenticed to rich squires to serve in the army. It is true, however, that in recent years the child has played a more proactive role in wars and now engages in actual physical combat. This tragic development has been partly brought about by improvements in weapons technology with the proliferation of simple and light arms which are easily handled and transportable by a child of ten (Faulkner 2001).

What makes children become soldiers is both simple and complex. Prime amongst the reasons is poverty, and that combined with the active recruiting campaigns of some armed groups and governments seem to offer some solution to desperate children. Richards (1996) argued that young people in Sierra Leone volunteered for their own clear and rational reasons, including survival, although others argue against this, saying that when the only options are death or desperate poverty, the word 'volunteering' cannot justifiably be used.

The impact of being a child soldier has been described by many as 'de-humanising'. The roles the children have to learn to play involve the role of witness to horrific acts; the role of collaborator in committing acts of violence; the role of partner with adults who may be brutal or threatening or themselves playing the role of father figure. Children are forced to become independent and to deal with things like dead and mutilated bodies,

burned out villages, acts of rape and assault. Feelings have to be repressed as there is little or no outlet for these. Children cannot express loss or grief or fear or loneliness.
Instead they have to construct some sort of protective shell or carapace to survive. These
children are effectively brought up by armed gangs or groups of militia who sometimes
act in loco parentis and become a sort of surrogate family. The future for these children is
bleak. They have no access to education and whilst conflict and war rage they have no
clear way out of their situation. There are efforts to rehabilitate these children ideally by
finding their families (where any survivors exist) or by putting them into institutions –
hardly an ideal solution.

For those of us in the developed world, with our industrialised economies, the notion
of children as soldiers is almost impossible to conceive of. However, it is a reality in our
world and one that reminds us that concepts of children and childhood continue to
change. Some of those looking at what has happened and is happening in places like
Sierra Leone state that it can be attributed to 'African cultural tradition'. This is a dangerous assertion and one that needs to be addressed. The use of children in armed
conflict is a socioeconomic event and often represents deliberate and pragmatic military
strategies. Twum-Danso (2003) argues that the use of children in wars is itself affecting
the cultures of the countries concerned.

In 2001 the Women's Commission for Refugee Women and Children set up a project
involving adolescents and adults in Uganda and Sudan, asking them about their experiences of living in situations where there was armed conflict. As you can imagine, their
findings were harsh. The adolescents said that the combination of war, displacement on
a vast scale, HIV/Aids, lack of facilities and development, and poverty itself created a
world that few of us can imagine. These young people were without the support of their
families and were drawn into becoming soldiers or prostitutes, of encountering sexual
and other violence and of having to act as the heads of households. They expressed very
clearly that what made things worse for them was that, despite them having to take on
roles that few adults could cope with, their views were still not sought, nor their voices
heard. They felt that they had the capacity, the competence and the capability to be
involved in the making of decisions that affected their lives.

Summing up

This chapter has adopted a rather different approach to the previous chapters, incorpo-
rating the writing of novelists and others in trying to examine the complexities of
children learning to play the many and different roles they have to play in their lives.
The issues addressed have included how children construct their gender identity and
their self-identity when they are out of the dominant groups. The huge variance in the
experiences of children's role playing in their lives is illustrated by the examples of the
street workers in Peru and Asuncion and the child soldiers in Sierra Leone. Our twenty-
first-century child may find herself playing some demanding roles in this increasingly
tense and often hostile world.

Questions

* What have you learned about how children use play to try out roles and explore role-related issues like power and subjectivity, action and passivity, anger and joy?
* Do the examples of children learning and playing more adult and difficult roles as street workers or soldiers allow you to think more carefully about the dangers of adopting the image of the 'everybaby' or the 'everychild'?

Chapter 8

The child as thinker
Questions and solutions

In this chapter we turn our attention to children everywhere, working hard to understand everything in their worlds and doing this without the need of specialist resources. We examine how aspects of the worlds that children live in raise questions in their minds or pose problems for them to solve. We see how children everywhere develop a range of strategies as problem-solvers and in doing this make hypotheses, try these out, analyse what happens, identify patterns, generate rules, use analogy, come to conclusions and move on. The problems children address range from very simple physical phenomena such as why things always fall downwards, to more complex things like why people fight, how people came to be living where they live, who makes up the rules, where the rain comes from, what it feels like to be powerful and so on.

Throughout this book we have come across children encountering things that interest or fascinate them and which sometimes raise questions in their minds. In Ho Chi Minh City we encountered Hung who went to the airport after school every day to sell his postcards to help with the family finances. There he taught himself English and in the process found people asking him what the time was. Using the big clock on the wall and asking questions as they arose he taught himself to tell the time so that he could answer the questions asked (and sometimes get a tip for doing so). In Lake Atitlan in Guatemala we came across some children watching their mother and older siblings making tortillas on the fire. As the young children watched the process, questions about why the dough had to be rolled and then flattened, what happened to the tortillas on the fire, and what made the tortillas taste so good may have been raised in their minds. We came across Louis in a school in London learning the multiplication tables and being fascinated by a trick the teacher taught him to work out whether or not the nine times table was correct. He then used trial and error over and over again in order to check up on whether his answer was, indeed, correct or not and from this was able to generate his own conclusion which identified the rules he had generated.

In all of these examples and in others throughout the book, the problems raised are real ones in the sense that they matter to the child. They are not decontextualised school-based problems – not even Louis's maths problem. In all the situations the children set about finding an answer using their own developing capacities as thinkers. In the case of Hung he uses the situation he finds himself in where he has worked out that learning to tell the time will be beneficial to him financially. The children in Lake Atitlan are learning through watching something that is an essential part of their culture and their lives. They watch, they listen and sometimes they join in.

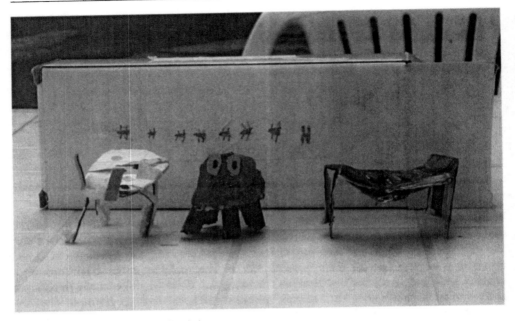

Ben and Hannah's home-made 'Zooks'

Ben encountered a problem when he was not able to make moving models of things he had seen on television and which required the use of a computer. Like many young children he addressed the problem by searching for what he could find – what Kress describes as being 'at hand' – and using what he found to make models. The picture above shows what he and his sister made.

Finding, using, making, evaluating

Kress (1997) regards all children as practised makers of signs in many semiotic modes. As children use the things they encounter to represent the world, they are exploring a rich world of meanings, made in countless ways. Kress regards this as essential practice for moving into the unidimensional world of written language. The signs that children make represent what they are interested in at the time. In the example above we see Ben – a child of changing passions – representing his interest in the moving online creatures he has been making on the computer. With no computer to hand he did not abandon his interest but transformed it and made a static model and alongside it he wrote out the instructions for how the 'zook' could be made to move if he had access either to a computer or to some batteries.

Pahl (1999) is interested in how children and particularly very young children in nursery classes express complex ideas through making things out of materials found and given. Very much influenced by the work of Kress she noticed how the making of models (and not necessarily realistic models) is much more than a mere cutting-and-sticking exercise, but represents part of thinking and ideas. Once the child has completed making the model the finished product then offers the child something to think about and allows the child to push their thinking further. In other words the act of making in itself is an engaging process which may challenge children's thinking and the finished product, once examined, raises more questions to be answered. The process appears to be:

- asking a question;
- attempting to answer it by raising a hypothesis;
- doing something to test the hypothesis;
- noticing what happens;
- confirming the hypothesis or not;
- coming to a conclusion or returning to check out the hypothesis in a different way.

What is happening is then a transition from one form of reality to another.

> Zethu made a necklace out of some seeds that she found and then threaded on some wire her dad gave her. (The seeds suggested to her that she make a necklace. She asked her dad to give her the wire.) She then needed to find a way to make holes in the seeds in order that they could be threaded on the wire. Her brother offered her a stick but it would not work. Her mother gave her a sewing needle which she used successfully. (She tried the stick and the needle to find which would work.) She then carefully threaded the beads on the wire and measured it against herself for a length that she liked. Her brother cut the wire for her and she twisted the two ends together as she had seen him do when making wire toys (learning from the model of her brother). She then sat back and looked at the necklace and decided that it needed to 'look prettier'. She found some of the paste her aunt used to decorate the clay pots and applied that to the beads, carefully, using a feather and a thin stick. When she had finished she announced that next time she would paint the beads first because it would be easier. (A reflection on what she had made – the product – enabled her to consider what she might do differently, indicating some of the learning that had taken place.)

Kate Pahl (1999) spent time observing the children in the nursery and some of her observations powerfully illustrate the complexity of the children's investigations into some idea that has arisen in their minds. Here are some of Pahl's examples:

> Lydia made what she called a carpet from some pieces of felt. She then selected an empty container which she called a basket and put the felt squares at the bottom of the container. In this way she had transformed the 'carpet' into a basket with a soft base.

> Lucy made a shopping basket out of an old tissue box. She made a handle for it and then wrote out a list which she taped to the basket. She said it was writing for her mum. Pahl's analysis is that she was linking concepts – shopping, basket and making a list.

Halliday talked about signs and specifically about how we represent ourselves to the world when we communicate. He mentioned three functions. The first was what he called *ideational,* by which he meant the way we say something about the world through an object. Then there is the *interpersonal* function, where we say something about the object's relationship to the world, and then there is a function which we have not mentioned before; this is the *textual* function, where we say something about the sign's form and composition – in other words we say how it is made. Pahl's analysis of Lucy's basket above is that the ideational aspects are the objects, the shopping basket and list, which both arose out of a shopping project in the nursery. The interpersonal aspect is the sign's relationship with the outside world and you will note that Lucy specifically did this in words when she talked of writing for her mum. The textual function is what the basket was made of. Lucy chose an empty tissue box and used masking tape and string. In the making of objects all three functions are at play.

In coming to understand children's representations it is important to remember that for the child there will be no distinction between the different ways of representation: drawing, writing, playing, constructing, making models and so on. For the child something – an idea – is the starting point for an exploration or an investigation and one thing leads to another. For Ben it may well have been the mobility of the computer 'zooks' that he wanted to investigate and when he had nothing to enable his models to move he went on to explore other aspects which had entered his mind during the making of the models. This is what we mean when we talk about the importance of children being able to represent and re-represent and it is important here to remind ourselves that this does not imply the necessity for expensive things. Ben's models are three-dimensional in form and he used a range of materials to make them, using what he found in the house where he was staying.

For both Kress and Pahl the signs that the children produce as they make models are intimately linked to their culture and their society and are also a precursor to literacy. Here are the children painting and modelling as ways of communicating their complex ideas before they arrive at literacy. It is worth reiterating that when children draw or paint or make models they draw on their particular cultural tools and their individual or collaborative experiences. Children making things in South Africa use what is to hand and make wheeled toys out of pieces of wire, dolls out of cornhusks wrapped in scraps of fabric, necklaces out of seeds threaded together and furniture out of empty crates. Children in Mexico are influenced by the icons and images they see around them and use sheets of thin metal, brilliant colours, skeleton figures and, in some places, detailed miniature versions of people and animals sometimes set in empty nut cases.

John Matthews is someone who has a passion for understanding what is happening when children draw. He was influenced by the work of Trevarthen who, you will remember, showed that newborn babies are able to take part in shared meaning making with caregivers, and tried to draw parallels between language and drawing in the sense of appreciating Chomsky's stance that children generate rules and use language creatively. All children make novel utterances when they say things that they could not have copied from anyone else. He believed that in the process of making marks, children also combined movements and sensations to produce new marks in their search for meaning. In his book *Helping Children to Draw and Paint in Early Childhood* (1994) he looked at the development of his own child, Ben, and asked if, when Ben scribbled, he was 'babbling with paint' (1994: 18): Matthews was keen to point out that those who are intent on assessing children as 'artists' do so against some notion of what accurate representation should be and in doing this they are using a culturally restricted and narrow definition of art which is Western European in origin and doesn't allow for artistic representations from other cultures including the use of pattern, of colour, of specific devices like dots in Aboriginal art and so on.

Sue Cox (2005) looked at children's drawing within the same philosophical and pedagogic framework as Pahl, Kress and Matthews. She observed children in a nursery where they were able to initiate activities and follow through their own ideas and she did not limit her observations to drawing (the making of marks on a two-dimensional surface), but also looked at children engaged in model making and painting. Her analysis of what the children were doing – the processes in which they were involved – is far from the traditional ways of looking at children's drawing in a Piagetian stage-type analysis. She is little interested in representation in the sense of the child being able to make something that accurately represents something else. There are a number of reasons for her criticisms of this approach to drawing; not least in that it is very culture-specific and open to judgement as 'good' or not. Cox seeks to understand what the *purpose* of the drawing is for the child.

For Cox, then, drawing takes place – as do all other expressive activities – in specific cultural contexts and is imbued with personal significance. Here is one of the examples she cites to illustrate this.

> 3-year-old Leanne was drawing with felt pen on green paper, on her own, in the writing corner of the nursery classroom. She began by drawing an enclosed oval shape. She then proceeded to fill the shape with dots, some of which, as her arm descended with some force, became more extended marks. As she continued, she began to talk to herself, unaware that I was listening (I was observing some other children at the time). She identified the shape as a duck pond and the marks she was making as ducks. She then made a final dot within the shape, and declared it to be the plug where the water goes out. She moved to the corner of the page where she made some individual shapes working from left to right. Reaching the edge of the page she continued immediately beneath. As she did this she said slowly, as she was making the marks 'To Auntie Bonny'.
>
> (Cox 2005: 118)

In her analysis of this detailed observation Cox noted how the child was ascribing meaning to the marks she was making and that 'reading' the drawing through the observed process gives some understanding of what the child's intentions were and how they changed as her movements and mark-making changed. Looking at the 'finished product' could not possibly have given anyone an insight into this creative process. Cox also illustrated in her piece how the marks made by a child can be changed as external events affect the child's thinking, and she illustrates this point by talking of a child who produced three arched lines and called them first a rainbow, but when a child close by sneezed, the child changed his label to 'a sneeze'. Transformations occur on different levels and children play with the marks they make or the models they create just as they play with words. A mark made in what might be regarded as the 'wrong' place can be explained by the child as part of a joke or a story or a play on reality. Cox is interested in the monologues she heard the children use (as in the example of Leanne above) and feels that they do not reflect the child trying to justify a drawing that is not visually accurate or pleasing but just to explore the same idea or ideas through another mode – i.e. spoken language. We are back to the idea of investigation or exploration involving different modes of representation.

Signs and symbols are not limited to those that are visual. All human infants are exposed to sounds from the moment of birth (indeed from before birth, as we saw in Chapter 2) and there is evidence that infants start to respond to music very early in life. Ilari (2002) notes that infants then start to produce what is called 'musical babbling' which is made up of sounds of varying length and pitch which seem to descend in melody but are not imitations of anything heard. You can see here the direct links to both Chomsky and Matthews. Moog (1976) was interested that babies at the age of about one year showed likes and dislikes, responding positively to songs and rhythmic words and also to instrumental music, but negatively to sounds like those of traffic or vacuum cleaners. Later babies begin to beat or tap or clap hands and join in with musical games. They also move to the music, spinning round, making stepping movements or dance movements. Hargreaves (1986) noticed that the songs children made up often contained a melodic phrase, sometimes made of three notes of different pitch. Trevarthen (1998), in his examination of how children need to learn a culture, found that mothers in many cultures sang to their children, danced for and with their children and exposed their children to the popular music of their time and place. He believed that children had an innate sense of musicality that allowed them to communicate with others before the acquisition of speech. Music, says Trevarthen, is a communal, cultural and communicative act. It does not require a huge cognitive leap to appreciate how important music is as a cultural tool and to recognise the diversity that exists between the music enjoyed by different groups, ages and cultures. Gardner (1973), who is famous for his work on the different ways in which humans learn, argued that there was a specific intelligence associated with music.

Beetlestone (1998) cites the example of five-year-old Fay, who was fascinated by the sheet music which accompanied her toy piano. The child asked many questions about how the dots on the paper could be translated into sounds to be made on the piano and through this began to see the relationship between the visual symbols and the auditory sounds. After a while she started making up tunes for herself, sometimes attempting to 'write' them down. In his series of Reith Lectures in 2006, the pianist Daniel Barenboim made much of the lack or recognition of the importance of hearing (as opposed to seeing) to learning and development.

When you consider how important music is in the everyday lives of so many people, it is extraordinary how little attention is paid to it in the writings about child development. What research there has been has treated music as being made up of discrete aspects – pitch, rhythm and so on – and has tried to identify the ages at which children show evidence of responding to these or recognising them. But music is much more than these aspects and further study of the processes children go through to make meaning from sound is needed. The only conclusion one can draw from what has been found so far is that infants are actively attentive to sounds and that the sounds they encounter will vary from culture to culture. It seems highly likely that children, offered opportunities to make their own music, will demonstrate exploration of different tones, rhythms, and patterns.

Why does this happen? What is going on here?

Greco (1962) tells the tale of how five-year-old Jean-Pierre solved an ongoing problem relating to his daily life. He lived with his mother and father and a sibling in Paris. Each day his mother would ask him to put out the table napkins for the main meal of the day. On the first day Jean-Paul started, logically enough, by taking one napkin at a time and putting each one on a plate before returning to fetch the next napkin. Here was a child depending on the concept of one-to-one-correspondence in order to be able to do as asked. He had to make four trips. He continued to make his daily four trips to set out the napkin for about three months. And then, one day, he decided to count the plates (he could count to 30) and then he counted out four napkins – and lo and behold, he only had to make one trip. He repeated this new pattern for six days but on the seventh day there was a guest for dinner and Jean-Pierre found there was an additional plate on the table. He took his four napkins in one trip as before, but when he got to the table he realised that there was a plate without a napkin. Dismayed by this he returned all four napkins to their place in the cupboard and then started all over again, this time making five trips to and from the table.

The following day the guest was no longer there, but Jean-Pierre made four trips to the table and continued to do this for five more days when he again reverted to his four-napkins-at-once method. Ten days later he was told there was, again, to be a guest for dinner. This time Jean-Pierre counted out his four napkins and then returned to the table to collect one extra for the empty plate. And on the following day when lunch was for his family alone he managed his four napkins in one go.

Jean-Pierre had to try out and evaluate his own solution to a problem which arose in the context of his everyday life. With no one to correct him he took a considerable amount of time, moving from one-to-one correspondence to being able to hold a number in his head, only to return to one-to-one correspondence when a new variable (the extra plate) required him to adjust his thinking.

You will remember Piaget's 'image' of the child as tireless rational scientist, trying to make sense of the world without recourse to context or other people. Those who argue against this see the world in which children live as simultaneously objective and subjective, meaning that there are things to explore in the world and that each person's exploration will be unique. So the child will make knowledge his or her own and will do this by internalising what is to be learned into what is already understood through cultural and collective knowledge. The implication of this is that children cannot come to make knowledge their own if they are required to integrate it into something of which they have no understanding.

Try this to see if you can make meaning of it:

> The afferent function of the non-specific structures involves branches from fibers in the trunk-line specific projection systems. Conduction within the non-specific system is to widely separated points, pooling the excitation from different senses, and the rate of conduction is slow. The cortical bombardment from the non-specific system therefore derives from all the senses indiscriminately.
>
> (Hebb 1958: 80)

Does it help if I tell you that it comes from a textbook about psychology? Or that it is in a chapter called 'The nervous system' and in a section of the chapter called 'Afferent, internuncial and efferent paths'? Presumably you struggled to make sense of this because it refers to things you have little or no experience of and hence nothing to help you on your path to understanding.

Bruner (1978) says that for a child (or indeed any learner) beginning to learn about something unfamiliar, the important thing is to find new and different ways of making sense of the world. Since we so often make sense by 'telling the story' (which is dependent on language), if we need to tell a story for which we don't have the language (the vocabulary and the concepts) we may have to find different ways of making meaning. When it comes to making sense of something in the natural world – something like physics, shall we say – Bruner suggests we need to find logical-categorical ways of doing this. So both narrative and logical-categorical ways of making sense are important since they prepare learners for the different domains of learning. Pramling and Samuelsson (2001) looked at how an adult (in their case a teacher) could move the child into a new domain by a careful and respectful focus on the role of specific language in building meaning-making tools.

They were looking at how a three-year-old child made sense of 'floating'. The adult had an array of objects on a table together with a bowl of water. The objects – there were ten of them – included a cork, metal screw and nut, pine cone, paper, fabric, and wood splinters. The adult asked the child if he thought each object would float or sink and why. The child then put the object in the water to see what happened. The first object chosen by the child was a cork. He put it in the water and when asked by the teacher said that it floated and when asked why said 'Cause it lays there'. The teacher does not correct the child but asked why it floated there (modelling the correct terminology). The child's response was 'Cause it is so very heavy'. You can see that the child did not understand heavy and light but moved on to suggest an alternative hypothesis – whether the object had a hole in it or not. The child had arrived at a tentative theory. Presented with a cork with a hole in it the child thought it would float until the water came in and then it would sink. The experiment went on with the child shifting explanations and thinking, replacing one hypothesis with another as his existing knowledge was challenged and then adjusted. The researchers believed that the child developed a discourse, which is a systematic process of inclusion and exclusion regarding what to say and what not to say, how it should be said and how not. They argue that the adult in this situation had allowed the child to make and test hypotheses and in this way introduced the children to how scientific knowledge could be discovered.

Our twenty-first-century child, as an active meaning maker, has been engaged in making intentional actions from before the end of her first year of life. In this way she demonstrates understanding of things before she is able to vocalise the idea or the thought. Shirley Brice Heath (1983) tracked what a small child, Vilgot, did in coming to understand what a book is and what it is used for. At first his actions and interactions depended to a large extent on imitation. At the age of 14 months he came across a book in his collection of toys, opened it, turned the pages and used oral speech. In doing this he demonstrated an awareness of *how adults make speech sounds as they turn pages*. At 22 months he responded to an adult's suggestion that they should read a book and chose a large novel. The adult sat with him on the floor, turned the pages and made up a story. The child listened, looked at the pages every so often and was quite satisfied with the whole event. This time his actions indicated that he *knew that a book meant hearing a story*. Four months later he picked one of his own books and handed it to the adult. The adult – Vilgot's grandmother – could not read without her glasses so she started telling it from memory. The child stopped her and instructed her to 'read it properly'. At that point he *knew that there was an invariant pattern to the book*. So he was aware of the text itself (what it was and what purpose it served) although he did not yet know the word 'text'. At 30 months he chose an older children's book and brought it to an adult who offered to read it to him. He turned the pages back and forth and then declined the offer, saying 'No, there is too much text in this book'; an extraordinary moment indicating that he had *understood what the word text meant and made a judgment that too much text meant that the book might be boring.* Just before his third birthday he asked the adult to write all the names of his family members and some other words using alphabet blocks. Whilst the adult was doing this he picked out and pointed to the letters of his own name, saying 'It's in my name' every time the adult used that letter. His *awareness was of individual letters.*

Children appear to focus their intention on what interests them. That is why play – the ability to explore something that interests the child in depth – is so important. When children display an interest in something it is likely that their existing knowledge or understanding about an aspect of the object or situation has been challenged and raised some questions in the mind of the child. For Vilgot, in Heath's wonderful case study cited earlier, the questions might include: What are these black marks on the page? What purpose do they serve? What are they called? What are these little black marks that make up the text? Why are there spaces between some of these black marks? And so on. It appears then that learning is the way in which children move from what is still unknown by using what is known. Each example of Vilgot's interaction with books shows him building on what he has learned in order to answer a question he has set himself about what he still does not understand. We might say that learning requires the ability to transfer a skill or a memory for use in a different situation or context.

Much of Vilgot's learning has come about through imitation, which may be one of the most important ways in which learners learn before language develops. A child can imitate by copying an action, internalise that in the form of a memory, and repeat it in a different context. Hay *et al.* (1991) believe that imitation in young children is not simply copying but a reflection on the whole meaning of the actions involved. So imitation has meaning because it reflects understanding of the intention of others. But is imitation enough to account for learning?

Imitation seems to involve also identification and elaboration. When the child imitates a person or an action the child is interpreting and creating something showing identification with an aspect of what is being copied. Vilgot at first imitates the saying-out-aloud-as-turning-the-pages behaviour of an expert reader and begins to act like or identify himself as a reader. He moves on from that to elaborate what it is he understands is involved in the process of reading. Elaboration means doing something personal with the imitation to transform it into something innovative. We see elaboration most clearly in role play where children coordinate and sequence what were originally imitations into elaborate continuous performances of a chosen role.

As you know, all learning and development takes place within a context and a cultural setting and it is this that accounts for variation as a factor in learning. The child, exposed to different situations, different objects, different interactions and different problems to solve, must first be able to distinguish one thing from another. In other words the child must become conscious of difference. Stern (1991), who worked with young children and their mothers, noted that all the small variations a mother exhibits when she interacts with her child strengthen the child's development of variation. Children learn what is appropriate where, with whom and so on. Variation is regarded by some as a key variable in learning (Lindahl 1996). We mentioned in Chapter 2 the work done by Athey (1990) on schemas, which are repeated patterns of behaviour. It is likely that children's repetitive exploration of patterns that interest them indicate their awareness of variation and it appears that the questions they might ask could include such things as: Will it remain the same if I do it like this? Here is an example:

> Harry has an interest in rotation. He draws lots of circles and spirals. He chooses round shapes when making models. He spins round in the playgroup. He holds a long ribbon in one hand and moves it in a circular pattern in the air. Perhaps he asks himself if something round will be round on the ground as well as in the air. Or perhaps if it will remain round when made with his arm or with a pen held in his hand or with a ribbon held up high above his head. Maybe he asks if a small movement will make a small circle whilst a big movement will make a big one.

This is a very straightforward example and we follow it with one drawn from Lindahl and Samuelsson (2002). It relates to a very young child called Wataru, who was 14 months old at the time of the observation and had an interest in spinning, which is very close to a schema of rotation.

> Wataru had just started at day care and he approached one of the teachers with a circular plastic ring in his hand. The teacher took the ring and spun it on the floor with her fingers. The child imitated the adult's actions, but not successfully. The child then put the ring on the table and tried to spin it there. It did spin a little. Later he crawled away, leaving the ring on the floor, but returned a little later with a ring with a large diameter. He crawled with the ring in front of him to show the teacher and he held it in the air to get her attention. She did not do anything with the ring at first but offered the child another toy which he ignored. But then the teacher made the big ring spin and Wataru took the small ring and succeeded in getting it to spin, at which point he hooted with delight. Still later he found a white tray which was circular and tried to get it to spin and when he was successful the teacher clapped her hands to confirm his success. Later still a little girl picked up the tray and ran off with it. Wataru tried to run after her but could not. The little girl teased him with the tray. A few days later he has a ring in his hand and the teacher has a tray and they are sitting in front of a mirror. He starts spinning the ring on the floor with great skill and he then moves on to spinning the tray. Later he manages to get a thick wooden ring to spin too.

You can see that the learning process starts with imitation but the child's passion for spinning makes him persist and seek to find out what other objects will spin. When he finds a circular tray he seems able to compare it in his mind with the ring that he could spin and later still he uses his memories of the spinning ring and the spinning tray to enable him to select the wooden ring. He was able to retain both his interest and his memory of what happened to allow him to explore spinning over time.

The rights of children: children's voice

Children's lives often present problems which range in complexity according to where the child is in the world and what their quality of life is. We tend to think that the lives of all children in the developed world are safe and secure and whilst this is true for some of these children the real facts are horrifying. In the 2005 review of child poverty in rich countries (UNICEF Innocenti Research Centre) it is stated that there has been a rise in poverty in 17 out of the 24 OECD nations for which data is available. At the top of the league table (meaning where there is the least poverty) are Denmark and Finland, where fewer than 3 per cent of children are living in poverty. At the bottom is the United States (the richest country in the world!) and Mexico, where child poverty rates are higher than 20 per cent. It is consoling to learn that child poverty rates in the UK have fallen, although the document points out that they started at an exceptionally high level in 2004. So there are children living in poverty even in the richest countries in the world and the impact of poverty on children is something they themselves are concerned about, just as they have concerns about their own capacities (as we have seen in Chapter 1) and about the injustices they perceive and the problems they identify.

> And it's like what my mum told me about Ireland. When the English people went there they said 'You have to speak English and you can't speak your own language anymore'.
>
> (Fiona, aged 7, quoted in Smidt 1988)

> You have to go to the supermarket and fill your trolley with tins and things that have come from South Africa. Then, when you get to the pay desk you have to take them out one at a time ... slowly ... and you have to look at each one and go 'Oh! I don't want this. This comes from South Africa'. You have to do it really slowly so the girl on the desk gets cross 'cos you're taking so long and then she will go 'We won't sell these things from South Africa anymore and that's because people won't buy them'. And then that supermarket won't have things from South Africa anymore. We really like red apples in my house but we won't buy them if they come from South Africa and my mum says it won't kill me to eat other apples instead.
>
> (Sam, aged 6, quoted in Smidt 1988)

Both of these children are expressing their thoughts and ideas about their perceptions of what is just and unjust, fair and unfair. These comments were made many years ago but give evidence that where children are invited to reflect on their own ideas they are able to use language (written or spoken) to help them communicate, clarify and sharpen up their ideas. This only happens where children are invited to think about issues of some substance. As Bruner (1986) puts it, the language of education, if it is going to allow children to reflect on issues as part of creating culture, cannot be the language of fact but must express some stance and invite those joining in to either agree with or adopt a different stance. This is, as you can imagine, a contentious stance because it allows children to think for themselves. Where this happens and children can reflect on what they think, they are involved in *metacognition*. This means that they are involved in understanding what it is they already know. Katz (1998), writing about what makes for high-quality learning experiences in the early years, agrees in the sense of wanting educators to address things that matter rather than those that are fun or trivial or superficial or phoney. An overemphasis on exploring meaningless topics and themes (which is often the case in schools) makes for not allowing children to explore and develop the very real issues that concern them. These include things like death and loss and war and illness and the dark and unhappiness and so on. Katz implies that young children need opportunities to express, improve, transform, validate, develop, refine and deepen their own constructions of their worlds – the world of here and now but also times past and times to come, of people like and unlike themselves.

You will know that children have rights and that these are stated in the UN Convention (1989). These rights include all categories of civil rights from economic and civil to social and cultural. Most significantly for this chapter, children are seen not merely as objects requiring protection but as participants with an entitlement to views.

The rights to life, to good health care, and to free primary education could not be questioned by anybody, but the right to require adults to negotiate with children is sometimes regarded with suspicion. Many claim that children cannot participate fully until they are capable of exercising responsibility and there is a general theory that young children are not able to express their own ideas. If you go back to reading about child soldiers and children working on the streets you will realise that children are perfectly able to hold views on complex issues and to express these through talk. Sheridan and Samuelsson carried out some research in 2001 with five-year-old children in Swedish pre-schools. They were looking at how well these very young children could use difficult terms such as 'decide'. The research was detailed and we will focus only on some selected issues.

The children were asked a number of questions relating to decision making. The researchers were interested in the responses given by the children and categorised them into groups. When the children were asked what they would like to do at school if they could decide, the majority of them responded by saying 'play'. This is, in fact, what most children do in Swedish pre-schools. The children were then asked if they thought that the teachers knew what they, the children, would like to do. To answer this the children had to have a theory of mind and this means that they not only had to know what they thought but had to recognise that other people (in this case the teachers) also had views and that these need not be the same as theirs. Most children initially said that the teachers did not know what the children like to do and when challenged and asked how they knew that the teacher did not know their preferences they gave a range of answers from 'she can't see us' to 'she isn't with us' to 'she is too busy' and so on.

The children were then asked 'What do you do when you decide something?' Their answers fell into several categories as follows:

- *To decide what you want to do.* This was the aspect of the word 'decide' revealed by the responses of most of the children. Their responses might have included statements like 'Well, we all decide we want to go outside' or 'We just start playing something and all our friends join'. Within the agreed chosen play there were almost always rules and the children mostly said that they either just accepted rules as given or agreed them together.
- *Allowed or forbidden.* Other responses indicated an understanding of 'decide' relating to what is allowed or forbidden. So one child might say to another 'You are not allowed to play with my doll' or explain 'We must walk in the corridor'. In the first example one child has decided what is forbidden; in the second the decision has been taken more remotely.
- *Aspects of power.* Here the children clearly focused on situations as where one child decides to play a leading role and then has the right to decide the rules – who can play, what part they play, when the play needs changing and so on.
- *Thinking out or inventing.* A fourth set of responses refers to the use of the word 'decide' as something creative. So children talk of deciding to have particular characteristics, for example, and use words like 'strong' or 'kind' or 'good at something' and so on.
- *To do what the majority wants to do.* The last category of meaning was given by only one child and came closest to a crucial aspect of democracy. The child talked about deciding to do what the majority wanted.

The theories of the very young

We have talked about how questions arise in the minds of children as they explore things that interest or excite them. From a very young age children seek to understand, interpret and later explain their responses to the questions they have asked. Some people are happy to call the questions children ask and the answers they suggest 'theories' and Rinaldi suggests defining a theory as a satisfactory, if provisional, answer. The answer is satisfactory to the child at the time. Through experience and interactions and more exploration, some challenge to the answer is made and the child then has to come up with a different answer. Rinaldi gives a wonderful theory given by a three-year-old girl, who said, 'The sea is born from the mother wave' and her analysis of this theory is worth quoting exactly.

> The child has conceptualised and is developing the idea that everything has an origin. Putting together all the elements in her possession in a creative way, the child formulates a satisfactory explanation, and while she is conceptualising it, she shares it with others.
>
> (Rinaldi 2006: 114)

Here are some other theories.

> Sandra, at the age of two, was taken to the docks by her parents and saw one of the metal structures that the boats were tied up to. She was intrigued by this unfamiliar object and set about exploring it – touching it, smelling it and walking round it. Then she announced 'I seed it and I feeled it and it's not a dog'. Her theory initially had been that it was a dog because it must, in some way, have resembled a dog. But upon exploration she realised her theory was wrong and she was sharing the challenge to her thinking with her parents.

> When Hannah was in the reception class one of the adults in the school wrote on the blackboard 'Maths is hard'. When Hannah's mother said 'I wonder why the teacher wrote that maths is hard', the five-year-old child replied 'She only speaks a little English so she doesn't know that it should say maths are hard'. Here the child's theory is that only fluent speakers of English will know that maths (because it ends with the letter 's') must be a plural and so the verb should match that!

The children in the previous section have all been expressing their theories, incomplete or provisional as they may be. Paying attention to these theories allows us a window into the processes children are going through as they come to generate theories and change them. As they pose questions and try to answer them they are exploring what is not yet known through what is already known. And what is already known comes from all their experience and their interactions. So their knowledge which has been socially and culturally constructed through interaction and exploration provides them with a set of internal representations which they then use to allow them to explore more deeply. Bruner talked of learning as following a *spiral curriculum* and what he meant by that was that the child will revisit something over and over again and that the representations will change with experience. Early *enactive* explorations will be dominated by senses and movement. Later *iconic* explorations will involve images and pictures. Finally, symbolic learning involves *symbolic* systems like language. This is a way of accounting for some of the features of learning we have addressed in this chapter:

- finding an interest which can be sustained over time or revisited;
- making representations which become internalised as memories;
- questioning, hypothesising and developing theories: answering the questions raised using the knowledge socially and culturally constructed;
- exploring variation, diversity and interests in different ways or modes; and
- experiencing challenges which push the child onto more creative, novel or sophisticated theories.

Summing up

We have tried to pull together some of the themes of this book in looking at how children learn. We have looked at some ideas on how children make sense of symbolic systems and use these to transform their understanding of aspects of the world. We have looked at how children develop their own theories and refine these as their understandings develop. We have looked at how seriously children can talk about important issues in their lives. In general the focus in this chapter has been on children as creative constructors and profound thinkers. Our twenty-first-century child adds to her repertoire the essential competencies of questioning, hypothesising, testing, analysing, generating rules, identifying patterns, making conclusions and starting again.

Questions

- What have you learned about how children reveal, test and extend their theories? Are you able to see them as brilliant thinkers?
- What evidence do we have of children – even very young children – being able to consider, explore and tackle extremely complex and difficult subjects – displacement, homelessness, prejudice, racism, injustice, poverty and so on?

Chapter 9

More than neurons

In this final chapter we turn our attention to critically examining what is being claimed from recent studies into what happens in the brain during learning. In doing this we examine the significance of the findings for children's learning and consider the reasons why educationalists seek to have a scientific explanation for what is meant by learning itself. We revisit some of the themes of this book – the importance of play, the issue of enriched environments and the prevailing myths about what constitutes quality in terms of parenting, learning, homes and childhoods. And finally we return to views of childhood in order to critically examine the impact of these on the childhoods of our twenty-first-century children.

> Zac is not yet three years old. He is learning rapidly and is intensely curious about everything he encounters. So he is asking questions about the physical world he lives in, and of the social world of his parents, siblings, extended family, friends, carers and others. He is using one thing to represent another and beginning to notice the patterns and the rules that apply when he hears people speak, or notices physical phenomena such as that things he throws in the air always fall to the ground. Recently he surprised and delighted his parents by using his knowledge of the word 'somebody' to create a novel utterance.' Somebody' is a word he has often heard used, such as when his mum says things like 'Somebody left the door of the fridge open' or 'Somebody is happy today'. Zac started using his brilliant invented word 'whatbody' to mean 'who' by asking 'Whatbody gave you that t-shirt?'

Science as a justification of learning

There has always been some way in which educationalists have wanted scientific back-up for their ideas about how children develop and learn. You will remember that Piaget's model was often described as a scientific model and that he was, by training, a natural scientist. You may have come across the work of Binet and Simon in Paris in 1905 who used a so-called scientific approach to develop and use a range of tests of the intelligence of children in order to identify those of 'low ability'. Chomsky, with his interest in genes and inheritance which linked him to the work of evolutionary theorists like Darwin, was often described as a scientist. Most recently – and perhaps most dangerously – neuroscience has been pulled into the debate and the effect of that has been the proliferation of some culture-specific and unsound so-called theories.

The desire to be 'scientific' in the study of children pre-dated Piaget and may have had its roots in the work of Charles Darwin. He was interested in child development and contributed something to our knowledge of it. It was through his work that ideas of child development became rooted around notions of biological universality giving rise to the concept of 'everybaby'. Darwin kept observation notes on the development of his first child William, born eight years after Darwin set out on his famous voyage on the *Beagle*. The notes in this developmental diary contain many thoughts about which aspects of William's behaviour could be called instinctive and which learned. Darwin was interested in how some behaviours remained in the repertoire of species and some fell out, and he believed that this allowed for the survival of the fittest. Darwin used much of his observational material in two publications: *The Expression of the Emotions in Man and Animals* (1872) and 'A biographical sketch of an infant' (1877). One of the themes of these works is that human infants quickly acquire the capacity to understand their caretakers and that this happens long before the acquisition of language. He believed that children's capacity to make meaning came about through their ability to 'read' the expression on the faces of others or to notice the intonation in their words. This is fascinating stuff and looks ahead to work done very much later. Darwin's writings triggered an interest in child development and resulted in the formation of the Child Study Movement which lasted for several decades, into the twentieth century. One of the features of this movement was that it claimed to be scientific precisely because it required the methodical and careful investigation of children by those trained in methods of so-called scientific observation.

The search for scientific backing for innovations in understanding how children develop is understandable. Often, official recognition and support together with money follow such backing. It is important here to remember that most of the work that has been done in the realm of science has been done with a small sample of the most privileged of the world's children. Yet, as we shall see, the findings from this small sample are being used by policy makers and funders for a succession of intervention programmes involving some of the world's poorest children and those most removed from the models of childhood involved in the sample considered. One of the findings relates to the importance of learning in the earliest years of life. This is nothing new, as indicated by the famous words of Ignatius Loyola, writing several hundred years ago: 'Give me a child to the age of seven and I will show you the man.' Loyola meant that the experiences a child has before the age of seven will be powerful enough to determine his (or her) future. We do know that early experiences are powerful and often influential but the question of how long-lasting they are is not yet scientifically answerable. LeVine looked at the issue through the eyes of an anthropologist and believed that the idea was largely rooted in Western beliefs and values, building on the work of people like Freud and Bowlby, who had a very particular views of children.

Sigmund Freud (1856–1939) is often called the father of psychoanalysis. In his work he looked at the problems adults presented to him, and situated the causes within the family and particularly in the early years of life. He viewed the child as an innately sexual being and saw sexuality in childhood as part of what he considered to be normal or natural development. At the time he was writing, sexual impulses were believed to arise only at the onset of puberty but Freud believed differently. His work has attracted attention over decades and is much criticised especially by feminist writers and thinkers who believed that he ignored evidence indicating the sexual abuse of children by adults.

Freud stated that children were sexual beings from birth. The behaviours exhibited by children – such as thumb sucking or playing with the genitals – should be viewed as sexual play and not ignored. He thus viewed childhood sexuality as being biologically determined and not socially constructed. He did not, however, talk about intentionality with regard to sex. To illustrate this he said that children may enjoy playing with their genitals because it feels nice but there is nothing to suggest they are aware of the sexual implications of these acts. You can see that Freud challenged traditional views on children and sexuality. You can also make some assessment of the view of childhood that he held.

John Bowlby had a background in medicine and was trained in psychoanalysis. He was interested in animal behaviour and particularly in evolution. His attention had been captured by some ethological studies into animal behaviour, most notably the famous study by Lorenz (1981) which seemed to show that baby geese would copy the movements of the first moving thing with which they came into contact. Bowlby, in his work with babies and mothers, felt that he observed similar patterns of behaviour in the ways in which babies bonded with (or, to use his term of preference, became attached to) their mothers or other primary carers. It was his belief that a baby would become distressed and resist separation because of this biologically adaptive mechanism which had evolved to protect the human species by keeping the young human being close to the mother. This aspect of his work has been criticised because it extrapolates from the behaviours of other species and ignores the personal aspects of bonding – those of communication and shared understandings. We know that in many cultures and societies there are different ways of child-rearing and bonding, different patterns of relationships and different styles of interaction. So Bowlby's work, whilst described by some as scientific, is very culture-specific.

His later work was even more contentious. Writing after the war, he was interested in the mental health of children and in their adjustment. He believed it essential for the young children to be brought up by the mother. His words illustrate this powerfully:

> essential for mental health is that an infant and young child should experience a warm, intimate and continuous relationship with his mother (or permanent mother-substitute – one person who steadily 'mothers' him).
>
> (Bowlby 1953: 13)

He was arguing for what he called 'natural' care and by this implied that any other care (by a father, a grandmother, in a group) was unnatural. The critics were vociferous in their condemnation of these views as being a reflection of Western cultural values and said these were being projected onto the children as being about the children and their needs. It is important to contextualise these views in light of the fact that he was writing after the war – a period where children had been in group care and women had been involved in the war effort. Tizard (1991) was one of Bowlby's most outspoken critics, stating that the strong emphasis on monotropism (which means the mother as sole provider of love and security) was an attempt to return mothers to home and kitchen and motherly duty. It is interesting that in 2005 similar views were being expressed in the media about how young children ideally need to be cared for by their mothers in their homes.

Valerie Walkerdine (1984) analysed changes to views of children at the start of the twentieth century and noticed that there was a growing trend to measure or assess them in some way. Walkerdine noticed that infants and children were weighed and measured at the local clinic or hospital. At around the same time scientists started studying the effects of such things as fatigue on children and then there was a growing interest in what the interests of children were. Their growth patterns were analysed and stages of growth plotted – years before Piaget began his work. Walkerdine believed that children were being singled out as a suitable group for scientific study. What followed from this some years later was children being singled as a group of potential consumers.

In the second half of the twentieth century a lot of attention was paid to the Perry High Scope project – a programme of early intervention in the lives of 123 very poor black children in the town of Michigan in the US. The stated aim of the programme was to improve the lives and the life chances of the children – on the face of it a very laudable aim which had its roots in the belief that poor children failed to thrive in schools partly because they came from deprived and impoverished backgrounds. Once the findings from brain research began to be published, those wanting to promote similar intervention programmes interpreted the tentative findings and used these as facts to persuade policy makers and funders. The reported successes of the High Scope programme included the fact that for every $1 of public money spent, $7 was saved through reduced criminality and other social factors. The findings from this well-intentioned but extremely small-scale project were extrapolated and became a sort of blueprint for the many intervention programmes that followed. In the UK the largest of these is the Sure Start programme with its intended aim of reducing poverty.

Over the past few decades, whilst neurologists have been working at understanding more about the human brain through technological advances being made in imaging techniques, educationalists and politicians have turned to their findings in an attempt to apply them to early intervention programmes. In summary, the educationalists have deduced the following:

- that the brain is at its most plastic and malleable in the early years of life –leading to the assumption that development during those years will last throughout life;
- that the connections made between neurons come about through stimulation – leading to the conclusion that, since stimulation in the early years will last forever and it is mothers and primary caregivers who provide this stimulation, they can be trained to ensure the child is exposed to an 'enriched' environment;
- that the synaptic connections made in the first years of life are critical in determining later cognitive abilities.

Bruer (1999) is someone who has thought deeply about these issues. In his writings he points out that the now-dominant theories about cognitive importance of stimulation are scientifically unproven and very culture-bound. He also points out that the brain research is in its infancy, has primarily been carried out on rats and monkeys and that extrapolating from these animal studies to human beings is insecure. It is his belief that the limited findings from brain research are being used by those with a political agenda wanting to use the arguments for early intervention as a panacea for change.

The human brain: fact and fiction

Fact 1: There is a correlation between synaptic density and intelligence

The human brain is an immensely important and complex organ, and information about it is being gathered through technological advances such as the use of magnetic resonance imaging and other techniques for actually 'seeing' what happens in the brain. You may have had a scan of your brain – a disturbing, noisy but painless experience of lying still as slim sections of your brain are scanned and photographed so that what is happening in your brain can be examined.

The brain is an organ that is hungry for oxygen and it is divided up into different sections. The cerebral cortex of the brain is the one that is most associated with thinking and reasoning and it, itself, is divided into two hemispheres that are interconnected. There is an ongoing debate about the different functions governed by each of these hemispheres. The cerebrum itself is divided in two halves and each of these is further divided into four lobes, each associated with particular activities as follows:

*   At the rear of the brain is the occipital lobe which is concerned with sight or vision.
*   Above this is the parietal lobe which deals with movement, number and orientation.
*   The temporal lobe is associated with hearing and language.
*   The frontal lobe is associated with feelings, emotions, planning and decision making, as well as with short-term memory and attention.

The brain consists of neurons which are sometimes described as the building blocks of the brain. These are so numerous that they have been compared to the number of stars in the galaxy. They are supported and serviced and repaired by an even more numerous set of cells called glial cells and these form a type of glue. What neurons do is to form connections or networks and the way in which they appear to do this is by sending tiny electrical signals along the axon (the body of the neuron) to be received by the dendrites (the arms of the neuron). Synapses are the connections through which nerve impulses travel from one neuron to another. The number of synapses relative to the volume of tissue is called synaptic density. There is some feeling that it is the laying down of these neural connections that constitutes learning.

Bruer (1999) tells us that the density of synapses in the outer cortical layer is not constant but changes through life. Human newborns have a lower density than do adults. But in the months after birth the infant brain begins to form synapses at an astonishingly rapid rate and these densities peak in all areas of the brain by the age of about four. They peak at levels well above those of adults and remain above adult levels until the onset of puberty when a pruning process seems to take place. The timing of this varies according to the area of the brain. For example, in the visual area synaptic densities increase rapidly from the age of about two months and peak at eight to ten months of age. They then decline to adult levels at around ten years of age. For the frontal lobe, which controls such things as attention, short-term memory and planning, the process starts later and lasts longer. Bruer suggests that synaptic densities change over the first 20 years of life in an inverted U pattern which he describes as low at birth, highest in childhood and lower in adulthood.

All of this is factual and not open to interpretation.

Fiction 1: There is a direct relationship between synaptic densities and intelligence

It is tempting to think that since we have the most synapses in infancy that we will ever have, we will learn most effectively then. In fact, it appears that although some skills and capacities develop soon after birth, most learning takes place after we have reached adult (i.e. decreased) levels of synaptic densities. Bruer tells us that we continue to learn throughout our lives and the more synapses we have tells us nothing about our intelligence or our ability to learn. Moreover, there is nothing we currently know that suggests that the more learning experiences we have during childhood the more we will be able to retain high synaptic densities and delay pruning. We cannot make our children more intelligent by 'cramming' in the early years.

> Joseph's parents were keen to provide him with the best possible start in life. From a very early age they read to him and told him stories and bought him books. Then they put up an alphabet chart in his room and every day his mother would teach him the sound of one letter of the alphabet. He then made a copy of that letter using play dough. When he went to school his mother told the teachers that he could read but the teachers found him unwilling to even look at books or listen to stories. When he was 16 he left school and went to work in a friend's café.

Fact 2: There are critical periods for the acquisition of specieswide skills and behaviours

You may have come across writing which discusses the importance of so-called 'critical periods' in learning. Much of the research around this has focused on the development of the visual system. Hubel and Wiesel (1977) showed that if cats or monkeys had one eyelid closed by surgical procedures during the early months of life the animal would not regain normal vision once the sutures were removed and the eyelid opened. They also showed that closing one eye during these early months had corresponding effects on the structure of the visual area of the brain. However, restricting vision in the same way on adult cats did not have these effects. It would suggest that only young animals had a critical period in their development that demonstrated this loss owing to deprivation.

Experiments of this type proliferated and there are three conclusions that most researchers agree on, as follows:

1   There were different outcomes from closing one eye, both eyes, or reverse suturing (which means opening a closed eye and closing the open eye) and this suggests that it is not the amount of stimulation that is vital during a critical period. What seems to matter is the balance and the relative timing of the stimulation.
2   Critical periods are complex and differ for different functions. There is a body of work on this subject, some of which indicates that for language, the critical period for learning phonology (the sounds of a language) ends in early childhood, but the period for learning the grammar of a language does not end until late adolescence. This may explain why those attempting to reproduce the sounds of a new language beyond early childhood struggle to do so, whereas learning the rules of a new language still seems possible.

3   Critical periods do exist and appear to have an adaptive value for an organism. It is generally accepted that as the result of the evolutionary process, some systems essential for survival must depend on the presence of environmental stimuli from very early on to fine-tune neural circuitry.

In summary we can say that critical periods exist and they appear to relate to specific abilities relating to the survival of particular species.

Fiction 2: Children need to learn particular things during critical periods

The emphasis of many of the programmes of early learning tells us that young children need to learn certain things before the age of seven. Bruer tells us that critical periods contribute to the survival of the species through providing for the development of essential skills and behaviours. Vision, hearing and language are species-wide abilities. All children (bar those deprived of everything and brought up in acute sensory depriva-tion – as, for example, in darkened rooms or tied to furniture or totally deprived of human contact) will learn these things. What homes or schools or pre-schools do will matter little to how children's sensory and motor systems develop. It follows that we have no basis for thinking that socially and culturally transmitted skills and knowledge (things like reading, writing, mathematics or music, for example) can only be transmit-ted during critical periods. Indeed it is clear that human beings can acquire these skills at any age.

> Rosie, at the age of 65, decided that she wanted to learn to play the cello. She wanted to make music with other people. She went out and bought a cello, joined a group cello class at an adult evening institute and within three years was playing in several amateur orches-tras, and chamber groups.

Fact 3: Complex environments in the lives of rats show that the brain can reorganise itself for learning throughout life

Neuroscientists have studied the effects of complex environments on the behaviour and brain development of rats. Complex environments are an attempt to create the condi-tions for laboratory rats which more closely mimic the conditions they might find in natural or wild environments. They are large cages, designed for groups of rats and where there are new objects to explore or obstacles to overcome. Greenough et al. (1992) found that young rats reared in these complex environments have 25 per cent more synapses or connections per neuron in the visual areas of their brain than rats reared in isolation. Some areas of the brain, however, show no effects. They concluded from this that there is no evidence for the often-quoted statistic that complex environments result in a 25 per cent increase in brain connectivity. (So here you have another fiction.)

More importantly, they showed that the brains of adult rats will form new synapses in these complex environments. This supports findings from other research (Nelson and Bloom, 1997) that the brains of monkeys and human beings retain plasticity and remain capable of extensive neural reorganisation throughout life. This runs counter to much of what you will read in education books and articles on the impact of so-called enriched environments.

Fiction 3: Children provided with enriched environments will learn more than those without

This is a serious and damaging misconception and one that has been and is being used by many in order to intervene in the upbringing and education of young children and thus offer them something specifically Western, middle class and value-laden. The use of the term 'enriched' implies its opposite of deprived and it takes only a small leap of imagination to see that 'enriched' might apply to what is on offer to children in California or Oxford or Cape Town, whilst 'deprived' might apply to those in Lima or Harare or Dakar. It is important to remember that complex environments have nothing to do with class or with the number of objects or with the cost of the objects. The vast majority of children are in environments that are complex and that offer them things to explore and hurdles to overcome.

Here are some examples of the environments in which young children find themselves. As you read them consider which, if any, seem to you 'better' than others in terms of promoting development and learning. The question is whether an environment that contains expensive objects will allow for better learning than one that does not.

> Sonya goes to a very formal nursery – a place that many parents admire because the children are expected to sit quietly, be polite, spend time copying things into their books and only going outdoors at playtime.
>
> Dumela, Sisi, Angelina and Hugo live on a farm. They cannot go to school because it is too far away and they have no transport. Each day they play outdoors with the things on the farm; in the evening their aunt reads them a story and they all have jobs to do to contribute to the life of the family.
>
> The children in Woodfall Park Nursery have three large rooms in which to play and learn. One room is set up as a home corner, equipped with beds and dolls and miniature household equipment; one room is a messy room where children can paint and play with sand and water; and one room is a construction area equipped with building blocks and construction toys.
>
> The children of the local village near to Hamburg all attend a day nursery and each day the children set out with the adults, each child equipped with a lunch box and a raincoat. The children spend all day in the woods, whatever the weather. They explore the things they find and make up stories and invent games.
>
> Pablo and Enrique go to the fields with their mother each day. They carry a small basket each – their grandmother wove it for them. They spend the day in the fields sometimes collecting things and exploring them or using them in the games they invent. They hear when the women take a break from their work and sometimes help with small jobs. As the sun gets higher they lie down in the shade and sleep. On the way home they listen to the women chanting and singing and join in.

No one wants to offer a sentimentalised view of the experiences of children. Some children lead lives of great difficulty, overwhelmed by poverty and illness, as in the dreadful conditions existing in many parts of sub-Saharan Africa. The majority of the world's children live in less than ideal conditions. But this does not mean that they will not develop or that they will not learn. The argument here is not that better conditions for development should not be looked for: the question is whether an improvement in the lives of these children can come about through intervention programmes based on Western views of children and childhoods and parenting and learning. Are intervention programmes a cheaper and easier and politically more acceptable solution than truly attempting to address poverty and inequality?

A final warning is issued by Bruer, who reminds us that, although brain research has had a relatively long tradition, we still have little understanding of the implications of the findings for the education, or for the learning and development of children.

Give me a child until he is seven

Loyola's words have acted something like a mantra over decades, with teachers and parents using the magical age as the cut-off point of development. So recent findings from brain research and the implications drawn from these have been added to the pervasive view of the importance of the early years for learning and development. The result of this can be seen in toy shops and book shops and websites in the developed world where parents and teachers are urged to intervene early in the lives of their children in order to enhance their learning. Books have been written and programmes developed urging this intervention. John Brierley was trained as a biologist and after a spell of teaching joined Her Majesty's Inspectorate and worked as a school inspector for 27 years. He wrote a book called *Give me a Child Until He is Seven: Brain Studies and Early Childhood Education*. The book is dedicated to nursery and primary teachers and uses the published evidence from brain research as though it is proven and universally applicable. At the end of the book Brierley comes up with a list of 21 principles. These include over-arching statements like 'What is well and soundly grounded in young children is likely to remain with them' and 'The years from birth to puberty are a crucial time when the ability to learn is at flood readiness' (Brierley (1987: 110).

A serious critique of brain research

In our criticisms to date of the interpretations of the impact of brain research we have focused on rather small-scale attempts to coerce parents and teachers to change aspects of the ways in which they interact with or teach children. Underpinning all this is the sense that those promoting the programmes have recipes for improving learning and development.

In seeking to critique current developments we need to return to the starting point of this book – to examine more critically some of the presumptions about childhood on which much of the research is based. All of these influence thinking and contribute to the ongoing divides between rich and poor, North and South, the developed and the developing worlds.

The first presumption is that childhood is a universal process and this is based on much of the work of traditional child development theorists who saw children as progressing from dependence to adulthood either through stages or phases, but in an ordered and predictable and rule-governed way – rather like other natural phenomena in the physical world. This allowed theorists to describe some things they saw as 'normal' development and, by implication, other things as 'not-normal' development. Add to this the fact that these theorists often ignore the sociocultural and economic impact of facts like family structure, cultural influences, power, status, economic levels of the family, and group and status on the development of the child. We have seen some examples of this even in the developed world where children in non-traditional family structures – for example single-parent families – are sometimes described negatively and perceived as being in some ways 'at risk'. Or as in cases where so-called childcare experts tell parents that young babies must be brought up at home, by their mothers, and not in any sort of group care. The messages this gives to those mothers who either need to work for economic reasons or to study are evident.

The second presumption is that adulthood has normative status, which means that children are seen as 'not there yet' – as being incomplete in some way, as they strive to achieve maturity, rationality, competence, awareness of society and their place in it on this journey towards adulthood. Adulthood, once achieved, somehow marks the end of the journey of development. But we have seen throughout this book that adults continue to develop and learn throughout their lives. The model here is of the incompetent child (or perhaps the not-yet-competent child) and this has been powerfully used as a 'scientific' justification for exporting Western models. The intention here seems to be to protect children from access to or participation in the adult world. In this model the incompetent children depend largely on the competent adults who are the ones to describe, interpret, explain and analyse the development of children. The real actors in the drama of their learning and development – the children – are passive and voiceless. Adults are presumed as knowing and right and children as ignorant and wrong. This is clearly a deficit model of childhood and one which allows children to be perceived of and treated as objects or possessions. Overheard on a London bus, on the New York subway, in a Johannesburg shopping mall:

> My daughter is not going to go to a state school just because I have some political principles. I will not sacrifice my child for my principles.
>
> He wants to leave school and go out to work but I insist that he gets some qualification.
>
> She is very sensitive and I will not have anyone insisting that she mix with children who have nothing in common with her. She needs to mix with her own kind.

The third presumption is that the goals of child development are universal and that these relate primarily to reaching levels of personal, intellectual, social and political autonomy, becoming independent and self-sufficient. Rational thinking in models like Piaget's is the ultimate goal. Yet we know that this is not the case in many cultures where such things as interdependence, collaboration and integration are highly prized. In most developed countries it is the adults who work and there is the need for an educated, skilled, creative, communicative, flexible and independent workforce. So children remain in schools rather than as part of the workforce and they therefore assume and are accorded less responsibility and a high level of dependence. But even in the richer countries, as we have seen, the childhoods of children cannot be seen as homogeneous and in these countries, as in the developing world, there are children who are involved in some way in the labour market. Where more and more women become involved in paid work, children relieve their mothers of some of the burden of domestic tasks. Lansdowne (2005) tells us that often the ways in which children's lives are played out is in relation to what is perceived to be in the best interests of the child. This sometimes provides a convenient explanation for the benefits of either children being in work (it develops their mathematical and social skills, their sense of self-worth and their status as a full member of the community) or children being kept out of work (they need protection and need to play and be free from responsibility). The ways in which parents structure the environments for their children are often in direct relationship to the goals they hold for the children. We have seen examples in this book, such as where we saw mothers valuing the ways in which children came to participate in cultural activities in Guatemala and Mexico, and Lansdowne cites other examples such as Japanese mothers wanting children to have developed emotional control, respect for their elders and some self-sufficiency, whereas American mothers expect to see such skills as empathy, negotiation, assertiveness and so on.

The fourth assumption is that children should be passive players. This presumption ignores the possibility of children being players or social agents in their own development and keeps children (and hence childhood) as separate from adults rather than seeing the extent to which children can and do influence adult behaviours and perceptions and can inform decision making and be heard.

The final presumption is, perhaps, the most far-reaching in its consequences on the world's children. This is that those who do not conform are in some ways at risk. This view, which pathologises children from 'other' cultures or minority groups, offers the rich West the opportunity to 'rescue' these children. The dominant view here is that schooling is good and work is bad and whilst we might all prefer children to be able to go to school and not to have to work, until the economic realities and divides are addressed, the majority of children in the world do work and they need to be viewed not as 'at risk' but as part of the world.

We know that governments in the developed world are investing millions of pounds or dollars in early intervention programmes which are based around many of the assumptions or presumptions that are listed above. Some use the evidence from recent brain studies to justify their proposals. It is true, of course, that many of them are well intentioned and no one is arguing against the provision of quality care and education for children. The issues are whether there is a recipe to ensure that all children will 'learn better' and whether those wanting to intervene possess this magical recipe.

In the UK, as in some other countries throughout the world, the cost of providing quality childcare and education for all children, including the poorest, is too high to be a real possibility. Much effort is spent in looking for cheaper solutions than the obvious one – the provision of universal childcare for all those parents who want or need it, offered by caring and trained personnel where the ratios of children to adults are low and the principles and ideas of the parents and carers are truly valued. There are some countries in the world where provision like this exists, but rarely is it free and the effect is that it is available for those who can afford it but not for those who cannot. In some of the richer countries, where there is an awareness that the inequities of provision maintain the divide between the haves and the have-nots, some intervention programmes to 'help' the poor have been put in place. Towards the end of the twentieth century there were moves in the UK to find some evidence that providing care and education for young children was something that would be 'good' for the children. This was when the eyes of politicians fell on the work of the neuroscientists, and the idea of a 'scientific' basis for the provision of childcare grew. It was at almost the same time that the World Bank developed its $1000 million loan programme for 29 countries to develop intervention programmes drawing heavily on the much-promoted model of the Perry High Scope Project which we mentioned earlier. The World Bank was arguing for programmes targeted at poor populations and the interventions were based on the idea of enriched environments. We need to ask whether what the World Bank is doing is to promote a social intervention programme into the lives of selected groups rather than trying to change the lives of poor children and their families in any meaningful way. Are the early intervention programmes nothing more than a panacea for poverty? Jerome Kagan, Professor of Psychology at Harvard (1998) certainly believes this, as illustrated by his statements that well-meaning liberals, who may certainly be interested in improving the lives of young children, cannot accept that early intervention will do nothing to actually alleviate poverty. The intervention programmes make them feel good and it is responses like this, at the individual rather than at the political level, that may well doom children to remain in poverty because such responses do not address the problem. Kagan was, of course, looking specifically at the US and argued that Americans have a desire to be seen as an open, egalitarian society, devoid of class boundaries, and that their interest in intervening in the lives of the poorest children in society does little more than create a smokescreen to hide the reality that they cannot face up to. Stephen Rose (1998), in arguing that social control is an underlying agenda in neuroscience, puts his cynical view very clearly: 'Science is about both knowledge and power. The new neuroscience is not merely about understanding but also about changing the world' (1998: 17).

In conclusion

Over the time of writing this book, during a year characterised by terrible natural and man-made disasters, millions of the world's children have witnessed or been touched by events too traumatic for most of us even to imagine. These have run alongside the day-to-day difficulties of life for some, and parallel to the joys of life for others. In the US, poor black children have lost their homes and family members just as poor Kashmiri children have in the high mountains and poor Guatemalan children in and around Lake Atitlan and hungry children in the creeping drought in Malawi and sick children in the depths of Swaziland. At the same time children in Toronto have been going with their parents to the cinema whilst Australian children have been swimming on the beaches and Greek children have been playing in the fields and Turkish children have been working in the market stalls and Chinese children have been flying their kites. They are all the children of this world and any account of development needs to remember them to ensure that the realities of their lives are reflected.

Questions

- In light of what you have read what criticisms, if any, do you have of the interpretations of some recent brain research which indicate that young children, if placed in 'enriched environments' are likely to thrive?
- Do you agree with those who feel that most of the world's children are in need of being rescued by those in the developed world?

Bibliography

Aarons, V. (1996) 'Telling history: inventing identity in Jewish American fiction', in Singh, A., Skerrit, J. T. Jr. and Hogan, R. (eds) *Memory and Cultural Politics: New Approaches to American Ethnic Literature.* Boston: North Eastern University Press.

Abbott, L. and Nutbrown, C. (eds) (2001) *Experiencing Reggio Emilia: Implications for Pre-school Provision.* Buckingham and Philadelphia: Open University Press.

Allery, G. (1998) 'Observing symbolic play' in S. Smidt (ed.) *The Early Years: A Reader.* London: Routledge.

Anning, A. (2002) 'Conversations around young children's drawing: the impact of the beliefs of significant others at home and school'. *Journal of Art and Design Education* 21 (3): 197–208.

Anning, A. and Edwards, A. (eds) (1999) *Promoting Children's Learning from Birth to Five: Developing the New Early Years Professional.* Buckingham and Philadelphia: Open University Press.

Aries, P. (1962) *Centuries of Childhood: A Social History of Family Life.* London: Jonathan Cape.

Athey, C. (1990) *Extending Thought in Young Children.* London: PCP.

Aw, T. (2005) *The Harmony Silk Factory.* London: Harper Perennial.

Bai, L. (2005) 'Children at play: a childhood beyond the Confucian shadow'. *Childhood* 12 (1): 9–32.

Bakhtin, M. (1981) 'Discourse in the novel' in C. Emerson and M. Holquist (eds) *The Dialogic Imagination: Four Essays by Bakhtin.* Austin TX: University of Texas Press.

Bakhtin, M. (1986) *Speech Genres and Other Late Essays.* Austin, TX: University of Texas Press.

Bakhtin, M. (1990) *Art and Answerability.* Austin, TX: University of Texas Press.

Barbarin, O. A. and Richter, L. (2001) *Mandela's Children: Growing Up in Post-Apartheid South Africa.* London: Routledge.

Barrs, M. (ed) (1998) *Part to Whole Phonics.* Heinemann.

Beetlestone, F. (1998) *Creative Children, Imaginative Teaching.* Buckingham: Open University Press.

Bergen, D. (2002) 'The role of pretend play in children's cognitive development' in *Early Childhood Research and Practice* 4 (1): 1–13.

Bialystok, E. (1992) 'Symbolic representation of letters and numbers'. *Cognitive Development* 7 (3): 301–316.

Bissell, S. (2002) 'Big or small, child labour and the right to education' in N. Kabeer, G. B. Nambissan and R. Subrahmanian (eds) *South Asia: Needs versus Rights.* New Delhi: Sage.

Blaise, M. (2005) *Playing it Straight: Uncovering Gender Discourses in the Early Childhood Classroom.* New York and London: Routledge.

Blenkin, G. M. and Kelly, A. V. (eds) (1987) *Early Childhood Education: A Developmental Curriculum.* London: Paul Chapman.

Bolle de Ball, M. (1987) 'Aspiration au travail et experience du chomage: crise, deliance et paradoxes'. *Revue Suisse de Sociologie* 1: 63–83.

Bolloten, B. and Spafford, T. (2001) 'Supporting refugee children in East London primary schools' in J. Rutter and C. Jones (eds) *Refugee Education: Mapping the Field.* Stoke on Trent: Trentham Books.

Bornstein, M. H., Haynes, O. M., Pascual, L., Painter, K. M. and Galperin, Celia (1999) 'Play in two societies: pervasiveness of process, specificity of structure', *Child Development* 70 (2): 317–331.

Bourdieu, P. (1977) *Outline of a Theory in Practice*. Cambridge: Cambridge University Press.

Bourgois, P (1998) 'Just another night at the shooting gallery.' *Theory, Culture and Society* 15: 37–66.

Bowlby, J. (1953) *Child Care and the Growth of Love*. Harmondsworth: Penguin.

Bretherton, I. (1984) (ed.) *Symbolic Play*. London: Academic Press.

Brierley, J. (1987) *Give Me a Child Until He is Seven: Brain Studies and Early Childhood Education*. London: Routledge/Falmer.

Brittain, V. and Minty, A. S. (1988) *Children of Resistance: On Children, Repression and the Law in Apartheid South Africa*. London: Kliptown Books in collaboration with Canon Collins.

Bronfennbrenner, E. (1979) *The Ecology of Human Development: Experiments by Nature and Design*. Cambridge, MA: Harvard University Press.

Brooker, L. (2002) *Starting School: Young Children Learning Cultures*. Buckingham and Philadelphia: Open University Press.

Bruce, T. (1991) *Time to Play in Early Childhood Education*. Sevenoaks: Hodder & Stoughton.

Bruer, J. (1997) 'Education and the brain: a bridge too far'. *Educational Researcher* 26 (8): 4–16.

Bruer, J. (1998) 'Brain science. Brain fiction'. *Educational Leadership* (56) 3: 14–18.

Bruer, J. (1999) *The Myth of the First Three Years*. New York: The Free Press.

Bruner, J.S. (1978) 'On prelinguistic prerequisites of speech' in R. N. Campbell and P. T. Smith (eds) *Recent Advances in the Psychology of Language: Language Development and Mother-Child Interaction*. New York: Plenum.

Bruner, J. (1996) *The Culture of Education*. Cambridge, MA: Harvard University Press.

Bruner, J. S. (1982) 'Formats of language acquisition'. *American Journal of Semiotics* 1 (3): 1–16.

Bruner, J. S. (1983) *Child's Talk: Learning to Use Language*. Oxford: Oxford University Press.

Bruner, J. S. (1986) *Actual Minds, Possible Worlds*. Cambridge, MA: Harvard University Press

Butterworth, G. and Harris, M. (1994) *Principles of Developmental Psychology*. Hove: Lawrence Erlbaum.

Cannella, G. S. and Viruru, R. (2004) *Childhood and Postcolonization*. New York: Routledge Falmer.

Carraher, T. N., Carraher, D. W. and Schliemann, A. D. (1985) 'Mathematics in the streets and in school' in *British Journal of Development Psychology*, 3: 21–29.

Chomsky, N. (1965) *Aspects of the Theory of Syntax*. Cambridge, MA: MIT Press.

Chomsky, N. (1972) *Language and Mind*. New York: Harcourt Brace Jovanovich.

Chomsky, N. (1975) *Reflections on Language*. New York: Random House.

Christensen, P. (1999) 'Towards an anthropology of childhood sickness: an ethnographic study of Danish school children'. PhD thesis, University of Hull.

Chukovsky, K. (1925 in translation 1963) *From Two to Five*. Berkeley and Los Angeles: University of California Press.

Clay, M. (1993) *Reading: The Patterning of Complex Behaviour*. Auckland, NZ: Heinemann.

Cole, M. (1996) *Culture in Mind*. Cambridge: Harvard University Press.

Cox, S. (2005) 'Intention and meaning in young children's drawing'. *International Journal of Art and Design Education* 24 (2): 115–125.

Craig. G. (2003) 'Children's participation through community development: assessing the lessons from international experience' in C. Hallett and A. Prout (eds) (2003) *Hearing the Voices of Children: Social Policy for a New Century*. London and New York: RoutledgeFalmer.

Cross, G. (2004) 'Wondrous innocence: print advertising and the origins of permissive child rearing in the US'. *Journal of Consumer Culture*, 4 (2): 183–201. London, Thousand Oaks and New Delhi, Sage Publications.

Dahlberg, G., Moss, P. and Pence, A. (1999) (reprinted 2004) *Beyond Quality in Early Childhood Education and Care*. London and New York: RoutledgeFalmer.

D'Arcy, C. (2002) 'Year 9 pupils teach at the University of Birmingham'. *Community Languages Bulletin* 11. Publication: 12923.

Darwin, C. (1872) *The Expression of the Emotions in Man and Animals*. London: Murray.

Darwin, C. (1877) 'A biographical sketch of an infant', *Mind*, 2 (7): 285–294.

Datta, M. (ed.) (2000) *Bilinguality and Literacy: Principles and Practice*. London and New York: Continuum.

Davidson, B. (1951) 'The Arts in Italy'. *New Statesman*, 14 April.

Davies, B. (1997) 'Constructing and deconstructing masculinities through critical literacy'. *Gender in Education* 9 (1): 9–30.

Derrida, J. (1972) *Speech and Phenomena and Other Essays on Husserl's theory of Signs* (trans David B. Allison). Evanston, ILL: Northwest University Press.

Donaldson, M. (1978) *Children's Minds*. London: Fontana.

Dunn, J. (1988) *The Beginnings of Social Understanding*. Oxford: Blackwell.

Dunn, J. and Hughes, C. (2001) '"I got some swords and you're dead": violent fantasy, antisocial behaviour, friendship and moral sensibility in young children', *Child Development* 72 (2): 491–505.

Dyson, Anne Haas (1993) *The Social Worlds of Children Learning to Write in an Urban Primary School*. New York: Teacher's College Press.

Dyson, Anne Haas (1997) *Writing Superheroes: Contemporary Childhood, Popular culture, and Classroom Literacy*. New York and London: Teachers College Press.

Ebbeck. F.N. (1972) Learning from play in other cultures. *Childhood Education*, 48 (2): 69–72

Ebbeck, M. (1998) 'Gender in early childhood revisited'. *Australian Journal of Early Childhood*, 23 (1): 29–32.

Egan, K. (1988) *Primary Understanding: Education in Early Childhood*. New York: Routledge.

Erikson, F. and Schultz, J. (1982) *The Counsellor as Gatekeeper: Social Interaction in Interviews*. New York: Academic Press.

Faulkner. F (2001) 'Kindergarten killers: morality, murder and the child soldier problem'. *Third World Quarterly*, 22(4): 491–504.

Ferreiro, E. and Teberosky, A. (1979) (English edition 1982) *Literacy Before Schooling*. Exeter, New Hampshire and London: Heinemann Educational Books.

Figueiredo, M. 'Tricks' in Smidt, S. (ed) (1998) *The Early Years: A Reader*. London: Routledge.

Flavell, J. H. (1992) 'Cognitive development: past, present and future'. *Developmental Psychology*, 28: 998–1005.

Foucault, M. (1979) *The History of Sexuality, Vol 1: An Introduction*. London: Allen Lane and Penguin.

Fox, C. (1993) *At the Very Edge of the Forest: The Influence of Literature on Storytelling by Children*. London and New York: Cassell.

Francis, B. (1998) *Power Plays: Primary School Children's Constructions of Gender, Power and Adult Work*. Stoke on Trent: Trentham Books.

Freud, A. (1965) *Normality and Psychopathology in Childhood*. New York: University Press.

Gardner, H. (1973) *The Arts and Human Development*. New York: Wiley.

Geertz, C. (1983) *Local Knowledge*. New York: Basic Books.

Gelman, R. (1990) 'Structural constraints on cognitive development'. *Cognitive Science* 14: (1): 3–9.

Glauser, B. (1997) 'Street children: deconstructing a construct' in A. James and A. Prout (eds) *Constructing and Reconstructing Childhood: Contemporary Issues in the Sociological Study of Childhood* (2nd edn). London: Falmer.

Goldschmied. E. and Jackson, S. (1994) *People Under Three*. London and New York: Routledge.

Goldstein, D. (1998) 'Nothing bad intended: child discipline, punishment, and survival in a shanty-town in Rio de Janeiro', in N. Scheper-Hughes and C. Sargeant (eds) *Small Wars: The Cultural Politics of Childhood*. Berkeley, University of California: Berkeley Press.

Goncü, A. (1998) 'Development of intersubjective in social pretend play' in M. Woodhead, D. Faulkner and K. Littleton (eds) *Cultural Worlds of Early Childhood*. London and New York: Routledge and The Open University.

Goncü, A. and Mosier, C. (1991) 'Cultural variation in the play of toddlers'. Paper presented at the biennial meeting of the Society for Research in Child Development, Seattle, WA.

Goswami, U. (2001) 'Cognitive development: no stages please – we're British', *British Journal of Psychology* 92: 257–277.

Goswami, U. and Brown, A. (1989) 'Melting chocolate and melting snowmen: analogical reasoning and causal relations', *Cognition* 35: 69–95.

Gottlieb, A. (2004) *The After-life is Where We Come From: The Culture of Infancy in West Africa*. Chicago: Chicago University Press.

Greco, P. (1962) cited in Williams, C and Kamii, C. 'How do children learn by handling objects?' *Young Children*, November 1986: 23–6.

Greenough, W. T., Withers, G. S. and Anderson, B. J. (1992) 'Experience-dependent synaptogenesis as a plausible memory mechanism' in I. Gormezano and E. A. Wasserman (eds) *Learning and Memory: The Behavioural and Biological Substrates*. Hillsdale, NJ: Lawrence Erlbaum.

Gregory, E., Long, S. and Volk, D. (eds) (2004) *Many Pathways to Literacy: Young Children Learning with Siblings, Grandparents, Peers and Communities*. London and New York: RoutledgeFalmer.

Gupta, P. K. (2005) 'India' in Penn, H. (2005) *Unequal Childhoods: Young Children's Lives in Poor Countries*. London and New York: Routledge.

Hall, S. (1992) 'What is this "black" in popular culture?' in G. Dent (ed.) *Black Popular Culture*. Seattle, WA: Bay Press.

Halliday, M. A. K. (1978) *Language as Social Semiotic*. London: Edward Arnold.

Halliday, M. A. K. (1993) *Explorations in the Functions of Language*. London: Edward Arnold.

Haq, Mahbubul (2000) *Human Development in South Asia 1999*. Karachi: Oxford University Press.

Hardy, B. (1968) 'Towards a poetic of fiction: an approach through narrative'. *Novel: a Forum on Fiction*, Brown University.

Hargreaves, D. J. (1986) *The Developmental Psychology of Music*. Cambridge: Cambridge University Press.

Harris, P. L. and Kavanaugh, R. D. (1993) 'Young children's understanding of pretence'. *Monograph of the Society for Research in Child Development*, 58 (1) Serial No. 231.

Harste, J., Burke, C. and Woodward, V. (1984) *Language Stories and Literacy Lessons*. Portsmouth, NH: Heinemann.

Hay, D., Stimson, C. and Castle, J. (1991) 'A meeting of minds in infancy: imitation and desire' in D. Frye and C. Moore (eds) Hillsdale, NJ: Lawrence Erlbaum.

Heath. S. B. (1983) *Ways with Words: Language, Life and Work in Communities and Classrooms*. Cambridge, MA: Cambridge University Press.

Hebb, D. O. (1958) *A Textbook of Psychology*. Philadelphia and London: W. B. Saunders.

Hendricks, H. (1997) 'Constructions and reconstructions of British childhood: an interpretative survey, 1800 to the present' in A. James, and A. Prout (eds) *Constructing and Reconstructing Childhood: Contemporary Issues in the Sociological Study of Childhood* (2nd edn.) London: Falmer.

Heywood, C. (2001) *A History of Childhood*. Cambridge: Polity Press.

Higonnet, A. (1998) *Pictures of Innocence: The History and Crisis of Ideal Childhood*. London: Thames & Hudson.

Hochschild, A. (2001) 'Global care chains and emotional surplus value' in W. Hutton and A. Giddens (eds) *On the Edge*. London: Vintage.

Holland, P. (2003) *We Don't Play with Guns Here: War, Weapon and Superhero Play in the Early Years*. Maidenhead and Philadelphia: Open University Press.

Hubel, D. H. and Weisel, T. N. (1977) *Functional Architecture of the Macaque Monkey Visual Cortex*, Proceedings of the Royal Society of London, B 198: 1–59.

Hughes, F. P. (1995) *Children, Play and Development* (3rd edn.) Needham Heights, MA: Allyn and Bacon.

Hunt, J. McVicker (1961) *Intelligence and Experience*. New York: The Ronald Press.

Hutt, S. J., Tyler, S., Hutt, C., Christoperson, H (1989) *Play, Exploration and Learning: A Natural History of Pre-School*. London and New York: Routledge.

Ilari, B. S. (2002) 'Music perception and cognition in the first year of life'. *Early Child Development and Care* 172 (3).

Invernizzi, A. (2003) 'Street-working children and adolescents in Lima: work as an agent of socialization'. *Childhood* 10 (3): 319–341.

Jalava, A. (1988) 'Nobody could see that I was a Finn' in T. Skuttnab-Kangas and J. Cummins (eds) *Minority Education: From Shame to Struggle*. Clevedon: Multilingual Matters.

Johnson, M. H. (1990) 'Cortical maturation and the development of visual attention in early infancy', *Journal of Cognitive Neuroscience* 2: 81–95.

Kagan, J. (1998) *Three Seductive Ideas*. Cambridge, MA: Harvard University Press.

Karmiloff-Smith, A. (1992) *Beyond Modularity: A Developmental Perspective on Cognitive Science*. Cambridge, MA and London: MIT Press.

Karmiloff-Smith, A. (1994) *Baby, It's You*. London: Random House.

Katz, L. G. (1998) 'Introduction: What is basic for young children' in S. Smidt (ed.) *The Early Years: A Reader*. London: Routledge.

Kearney, C. (2003) *The Monkey's Mask: Identity, Memory, Narrative and Voice*. Stoke on Trent: Trentham Books.

Kenner, C. (2000) 'Symbols make text: a social semiotic analysis of writing in a multilingual nursery'. *Written Language and Literacy*, 3 (2): 235–266.

Kenner, C. (2004a) 'Community School pupils reinterpret their knowledge of Chinese and Arabic for primary school peers' in Gregory, E., Long, S and Volk, D. (eds) (2004) *Many Pathways to Literacy: Young Children Learning with Siblings, Grandparents, Peers and Communities*. London and New York: RoutledgeFalmer.

Kenner, C. (2004b) *Becoming Biliterate: Young Children Learning Different Writing Systems*. Stoke on Trent: Trentham Books.

Kenner, C. and Kress, G. (2003) 'The multisemiotic resources of biliterate children'. *Journal of Early Childhood Literacy* 3 (2): 179–202.

Kenner, C., Kress, G., Al-Khatib, H., Kam, R. and Tsai, K.-C. (2004) 'Finding the keys to biliteracy: how young children interpret different writing systems'. *Language and Education* 18 (2): 124–144.

Kramsch, C. (ed.) (2002) *Language Acquisition and Language Socialization: Ecological Perspectives*. London and New York: Continuum.

Kress, G. (1997) *Before Writing: Rethinking the Paths to Literacy*. London: Routledge.

Kress, G. (2000) *Early Spelling: Between Convention and Creativity*. London: Routledge.

Lamb, M. (1999) *Parenting and Child Development in 'Non-Traditional' Families*. New Jersey: Lawrence Erlbaum.

Lansdowne, G. (2005) *The Evolving Capacities of the Child*. UNICEF Innocenti Research Centre.

Lash, S. and Urry, J. (1994) *Economies of Sign and Space*. London: Sage.

Lave, J. and Wenger, E. (1991) *Situated Learning: Legitimate Peripheral Participation*. Cambridge: Cambridge University Press.

Levi, P. (1979) *The Truce*. London: Abacus.

Levi, P. (1988) *The Drowned and the Saved*. London: Michael Joseph.

LeVine, R. A., LeVine, S., Liedermann, P. H., Brazelton, T. B., Dixon, S., Richman, A. and Keffer, C. H. (1994) *Child Care and Culture: Lessons from Africa*. Cambridge: Cambridge University Press.

LeVine, R. (2003) *Childhood Socialization: Comparative Studies of Parenting, Learning and Educational Change*. Hong Kong: Comparative Education Research Centre.

Lindahl, M. (1996) *Experience and Learning*. Gothenburg (in Swedish but cited in Lindahl, M. and Samuelsson, 2002).

Lindahl. M. and Samuelsson, I. P. (2002) 'Imitation and variation: reflections on toddlers' strategies for learning'. *Scandinavian Journal of Education Research* 46 (1).

Lloyd, B. and Duveen, G. (1990) 'A semiotic analysis of the development of social representations of gender' in B. Lloyd and G. Duveen (eds) *Social Representations and the Development of Knowledge*. Cambridge: Cambridge University Press.

Lofdahl, A. (2005) '"The funeral": a study of children's shared meaning-making and its developmental significance'. *Early Years* 25 (1): 5–16.

Lorenz, K. (1981) *The Foundations of Ethnology*. New York: Springer-Verlag.

Luo, Y., Baillargeon, R., Brueckner, L. and Munakata, Y. (2003) 'Reasoning about a hidden object after a delay: evidence for robust representations in 5-month-old infants'. *Cognition*, 878 (3): B23–32.

Marsh. J. and Millard, E. (2000) *Literacy and Popular Culture: Using Children's Culture in the Classroom*. London: PCO.

Mayall, B., Bendelow, G., Storey, P. and Veltman, M. (1996) *Children's Health in Primary Schools*. London: Falmer Press.

Mayall. B. (1999) 'Children in action at home and in school' in M. Woodhead, D. Faulkner and K. Littleton (eds) *Making Sense of Social Development*. London: Routledge.

Mayall, B. (2000) 'Negotiating childhoods'. *ESRC Children 5–16 Research Briefing*, No. 13, April.

Matthews, J. (1997) 'The 4 Dimensional Language of Infancy: The Interpersonal Basis of Art Practice'. *International Journal of Art and Design Education* 16 (3): 285–293.

Matthews, J. (1994) *Helping Children to Draw and Paint in Early Childhood*. London: Hodder & Stoughton.

McIvor, C. (1995) 'Children and disability: rights and participation' in SCF, *In our Own Words: Disability and Integration in Morocco*. London: Save the Children.

Meadows, S. (1993) *The Child as Thinker: The Development and Acquisition of Cognition in Childhood*. London and New York: Routledge.

Meltzoff, A. N. and Gopnick, A. (1993) 'The role of imitation in understanding persons and developing theories of mind' in S. Baron-Cohen, H. Tager-Flusberg and D. Cohen (eds) *Understanding Other Minds: Perspectives from Autism*. New York: Oxford University Press.

Moog, H. (1968) (English Translation 1976) *The Musical Experience of the Pre-school Child*. London: Schott Music.

Moyles, J. (1988) *Just Playing? The Role and Status in Play in Early Childhood Education*. Milton Keynes: Open University Press.

Moyles, J. (1998) 'To play or not to play? That is the question!' in S. Smidt (ed.) *The Early Years: A Reader*. London: Routledge.

Nelson, C. A. and Bloom, F. E. (1997) 'Child development and neuroscience' in *Child Development* 68 (5): 970–987.

Nelson, K. (2000) 'Narrative, time and the emergence of the encultured self'. *Culture and Psychology* 6 (2): 183–196.

Nsamenang, A. Bame and Lamb, M. E. (1994) 'Socialization of Nso children in the Bamenda Grassfields of Northwest Cameroon' in M. Woodhead, D. Faulkner and K. Littleton (eds) *Cultural Worlds of Early Childhood*. London and New York: Routledge and The Open University.

Oates, J. (ed.) (1994) *The Foundations of Child Development*. Milton Keynes and Oxford: The Open University with Blackwell.

O'Kane, C. (2002) 'Marginalised children as social actors for social justice in South Asia'. *British Journal of Social Work* 32: 697–710.

Oxley, J., Thai-Than, D. and Antolin, P. (2000) 'Poverty dynamics in six OECD countries'. *OECD Studies* 30 (8): 7–52.

Pahl, K. (1999) *Transformation: Meaning Making in Nursery Education*. Stoke on Trent: Trentham Books.

Painter, C. (1999) *Learning Through Language in Early Childhood*. London and New York: Cassell.

Paley, V. G. (1984) *Boys and Girls: Superheroes in the Doll Corner*. Chicago, IL: University of Chicago Press.

Penn, H. (2001) 'Research in the majority world' in T. David (ed.) *Promoting Evidence-Based Practice in Early Childhood Education: Research and its Implications*. London: JAI (289–302).

Penn, H. (2005) *Unequal Childhoods: Young Children's Lives in Poor Countries*. London and New York: Routledge.

Piaget, J. (1962) *Play, Dreams and Imitation in Childhood*. London: Routledge and Kegan Paul.

Piaget, J. (1970) *Structuralism*. New York: Basic Books.

Pinker. S (1994) *The Language Instinct*. London: Penguin.

Pinker, S. (2002) *The Blank Slate: The Modern Denial of Human Nature*. London: Penguin.

Pramling, N. and Samuelsson, I. G. (2001) "'It is floating 'cause there is a hole'": a young child's experience of natural science' *Early Years*, 21 (2): 139–49.

Prout, A. and James, A. (1990/1997) 'A new paradigm for the sociology of childhood. Provenance, promise and problems' in A. James and A. Prout (eds) *Constructing and Reconstructing Childhood: Contemporary Issues in the Sociological Study of Childhood* (2nd edn) London: Falmer Press.

Prout, J. (2005) *The Future of Childhood*. Abingdon, NY: RoutledgeFalmer.

Rahnema, M. and Bawtree, V. (eds) (1997) *The Post-Development Reader*. London and New York: Zed Books.

Raman, V. (2000) *Childhood – Western and Indian: An Exploratory Essay*. New Delhi: Centre for Women's Development Studies.

Reddy, N. (2000) 'Children as partners in change: children, citizenship and governance'. Unpublished keynote address at the Baspcan Congress, York, September.

Richards, P. (1996) *Fighting in the Rain Forest: War, Youth and Resources in Sierra Leone*. The International Association of African Affairs: Oxford.

Richter, L. and Griesel, R. (1994) 'Malnutrition, low birth weight and related influences on psychological development' in A. Dawes and D. Donald (eds) *Childhood and Adversity: Psychological Perspectives from South African Research*. Cape Town: David Philip.

Rinaldi, C. (2006) *In Dialogue with Reggio Emilia: Listening, Researching and Learning*. London and New York: Routledge.

Rogoff, B. (1990) *Apprenticeship in Thinking: Cognitive Development in Social Context*. Oxford, Oxford University Press.

Rogoff, B. (2003) *The Cultural Nature Of Development*. Oxford: Oxford University Press.

Rogoff, B *et al.* (1993) 'Guided participation in cultural activities by toddlers and caregivers'. Monogram Social Research. *Child Development* 58 (7) Ser. No. 236.

Romero, M. E. (2004) 'Cultural literacy in the world of Pueblo children' in E. Gregory, S. Long and D. Volk (eds) *Many Pathways to Literacy: Young Children Learning with Siblings, Grandparents, Peers and Communities*. London and New York: RoutledgeFalmer.

Roopnarine, J. L., Johnson, J. E. and Hooper, F. H. (eds) (1994) *Children's Play in Diverse Cultures*. Albany, NY: State University of New York Press.

Rose, S. (ed.) (1998) *From Brains to Consciousness? Essays on the New Science of the Mind*. London: Penguin.

Russ, S. W. and Kaugars, A. S. (1999) 'Emotion in children's play and creative problem solving'. *Creativity Research Journal*, 13 (2): 211–219.

Rosemberg, F. (2005) 'Ruthless rhetoric: child and youth prostitution in Brazil'. *Childhood* 6 (1): 113–131.

Rosen, H. (1984) *Stories and Meanings*. Sheffield, UK: NATE.

Roskos, K. A. and Christie, J. F. (eds) (2000) *Play and Literacy in Early Childhood: Research from Multiple Perspectives*. Mahwah, NJ: Lawrence Erlbaum Associates.

Rousseau, J. J. (orig. 1762, edition 2000) *Emile*, London: Penguin.

Rutter. J. and Jones, C. (eds) (2001) *Refugee Education: Mapping the Field*. Stoke on Trent: Trentham Books.

Sarangi, S. and Roberts, C. (2002) 'Discourse (mis)alignments in professional gatekeeping encounters' in C. Candlin and S. Sarangi (eds) *Language Acquisition and Language Socialization: Ecological Perspectives*. London and New York: Continuum.

Sassoon, A. S. (1987) *Gramsci's Politics* (2nd edn). London: Hutchinson.

Sayeed, Z. and Guerin, E. (2000) *Early Years Play: A Happy Medium for Assessment and Intervention*. London: David Fulton.

Scheper-Hughes, M. (1993) *Death Without Weeping: The Violence of Everyday Life in Brazil*. Berkeley: University of California Press.

Segall, M. H., Dasen, P. R., Berry, J. W. and Poortinga, Y. H. (1990) *Human Behaviour in Global Perspectives*. New York: Pergamon.

Shahar, S. (1990) *Childhood in the Middle Ages*. London: Routledge.

Sheridan, S. and Samuelsson, I. P. (2001) 'Children's conceptions of participation and influence in pre-school: a perspective on pedagogical quality'. *Contemporary Issues in Early Childhood* 2 (2).

Silin, J. G. (1995) *Sex, Death and the Education of Children: Our Passion for Ignorance in the Age of AIDS*. New York: Teachers College Press.

Skuttnab-Kangas, T. and Cummins, J. (eds) (1988) *Minority Education: From Shame to Struggle*. Clevedon: Multilingual Matters.

Smidt, S. (1988) 'Making links: children talking about reality'. *English in Education* 22 (1), National Association for the Teaching of English.

Smidt, S. (ed.) (1998) *The Early Years: A Reader*. London: Routledge.

Smidt, S. (2001) '"All stories that have happy endings, have a bad character": a young child responds to televisual texts'. *English in Education* 35 (2).

Smidt, S. (2004) 'Sinister storytellers, magic flutes and spinning tops: the links between play and "popular" culture'. *Early Years* 24 (1).

Smilansky, S. (1968) *The Effects of Sociodramatic Play on Preschool Children*. New York. John Wiley and Sons, Inc.

Smilansky, S. and Shefataya, L. (1990) *Facilitating Play: A Medium for Promoting Cognitive, Socio-emotional and Economic Development in Young Children*. Silver Springs, MD: Psychosocial and Educational Publications.

Stern, D. (1991) 'A young child's diary' (in Swedish) cited in M. Lindahl and I. P. Samuelsson (2002) 'Imitation and variation: reflections on toddlers' strategies for learning' *Scandinavian Journal of Educational Research* 46 (1).

Super, C. M. and Harkness, S. (1986) 'The developmental niche: a conceptualisation at the interface of child and culture'. *International Journal of Behavioural Development* 9: 545–569.

Suzlby, E. (1986) 'Writing and reading: signs of written and oral language organization in the young child' in W. Teale and E. L. Sulzby (eds) *Emergent Literacy: Writing and Reading*. Norwood, NJ: Ablex.

Theis, J. (2001) 'Tools for child rights programming: a training manual'. Save the Children (unpublished).

Tizard, B. (1991) 'Working mothers and the care of young children' in A. Phoenix and A. Woollett (eds) *Social Construction of Motherhood*. London: Sage.

Tobin, J. J. (1997) *Playing Doctors in Two Cultures: The United States and Ireland*. New Haven, CT: Yale University Press.

Tomasello, M. (1997) 'Joint attention as social cognition' in C. D. Moore and P. Dunham (eds) *Joint Attention: Its Origins and Role in Development*. Hillsdale: Erlbaum.

Tomasello, M. and Rakoczy, H. (2003) 'What makes human cognition unique? from individual to shared to collective intentionality'. *Mind and Language* 18 (2): 121–147.

Tomasello, M., Striano, T. and Rochat, P. (1999) 'Do young children use objects as symbols'. *British Journal of Developmental Psychology* 17: 563–584.

Trevarthen, C. (1977) 'Descriptive analyses of infant communicative behaviour' in H. R. Schaffer (ed.) *Studies in Mother–Infant Interaction*. London: Academic Press.

Trevarthen, C. (1998) (originally 1995) 'The child's need to learn a culture' in M. Woodhead, D. Faulkner and K. Littleton (eds) *Cultural Worlds of Early Childhood*. London and New York: Routledge and The Open University.

Twum-Danso, A. (2003) 'Africa's young soldiers: The co-option of childhood'. *Monograph* no. 82. Accessed 31 May 2006 at www.iss.co.za/Pubs/Monographs/No82/Intro.html

UNICEF (2000) *The State of the World's Children 2000*. New York: UNICEF.

UNICEF (2005) *Child Poverty in Rich countries 2005*. Florence, UNICEF Innocenti Research Centre.

Viruru, R. (2001) *Early Childhood Education: Postcolonial Perspectives from India*. London: Sage.

Volosinov, B. (1973) *Marxism and the Philosophy of Language*. New York: Seminar Press.

Vygotsky, L. S. (1962) *Thought and Language*. Cambridge, MA: MIT Press.

Vygotsky, L. S. (1966) 'Play and its role in the mental development of the child'. *Soviet Psychology*, 12 (6): 62–76.

Vygotsky, L. S. (1978) *Mind in Society: The Development of Higher Psychological Processes*. Cambridge: Harvard University Press.

Vygotsky, L. S. (1981) 'The instrumental method in psychology' In J. V. Wertsch (ed.) *The Concept of Activity in Soviet Psychology*. Armonk, NY: M. E. Sharpe.

Walkerdine, V. (1984) 'Developmental psychology and the child-centred pedagogy: the insertion of Piaget's theory into primary school practice' in J. Henriques, W. Hollway, C. Urwin, C. Venn and Walkerdine, V. (eds) *Changing the Subject*. London: Methuen.

Walkerdine, V. (1988) *The Mastery of Reason: Cognitive Development and the Production of Rationality*. London: Routledge.

Wertsch, J.V. and Stone, C.A. (1979) 'A social interactional analysis of learning disabilities remediation'. Paper presented at International Conference of Assessment for Children with Learning Difficulties, San Francisco.

Wertsch, J. V. and Stone, C. A. (1985) 'The concept of internalisation in Vygotsky's account of the genesis of higher mental functions' in J. V. Wertsch (ed.) *Culture, Communication and Cognition*. Cambridge: Cambridge University Press.

White, S. (2001) *Child Brigade: An Organisation of Street Working Children in Bangladesh*. Dhaka and University of Bath UK: Save the Children, Sweden.

Whitehead, M. (1997) *Language and Literacy in the Early Years* (2nd edn). London: Paul Chapman.

Williams, A. (2004) 'Playing school in multiethnic London' in E. Gregory, S. Long and D. Volk (eds) (2004) *Many Pathways to Literacy: Young Children Learning with Siblings, Grandparents, Peers and Communities*. London and New York: RoutledgeFalmer.

Winterson, J. (1985) *Oranges are Not the Only Fruit*. London, Boston, Melbourne and Henley: Pandora Press.

Woodhead, M. (1997) 'Psychology and the cultural construction of children's needs' in A. James and A. Prout (eds) *Constructing and Reconstructing Childhood: Contemporary Issues in the Sociological Study of Childhood* (2nd edn). London: Falmer.

Woodhead, M., Faulkner, D. and Littleton, K. (eds) (1998) *Cultural Worlds of Early Childhood*. London: Routledge with the Open University.

Author index

Subject index

Lightning Source UK Ltd.
Milton Keynes UK
17 November 2010

162962UK00006B/7/P

9 780415 385701